# Bill Oddie's
# BIRDS
## OF BRITAIN & IRELAND

This reprint published in 2004
First published in 1998 by
New Holland Publishers (UK) Ltd
London • Cape Town • Sydney • Singapore

Garfield House, 86-88 Edgware Road, London W2 2EA, United Kingdom
www.newhollandpublishers.com

80 McKenzie Street, Cape Town 8001, South Africa

14 Aquatic Drive, Frenchs Forest, NSW 2086, Australia

218 Lake Road, Northcote, Auckland, New Zealand

9 10 8

ISBN 1 85368 488 0

Publishing Manager: Jo Hemmings
Editor: Sylvia Sullivan
Designer: Alan Marshall
Artwork: David Daly, Stephen Message, Clive Byers, (as credited below)
Index: Sylvia Sullivan

Typeset by Alan Marshall
Reproduction by cmyk, South Africa
Printed and bound in Singapore by Tien Wah Press (Pte) Ltd

ARTWORK CREDITS

David Daly: title page, 6, 22, 23, 24, 25, 26, 27, 28, 29, 30, 31, 32, 33, 34, 35, 36, 37, 38, 39, 40, 41,
42, 43, 44, 45, 46, 47, 48, 49, 50, 51, 52, 53, 58, 59, 60, 61, 62, 70, 71, 72, 75, 76, 77, 112, 113,
114, 115, 116, 117, 118, 119, 132, 133, 134, 135, 136, 137, 138, 139, 140, 141, 142, 143, 144, 145,
146, 147, 148, 149, 150, 151, 152, 153, 154, 155, 156, 157, 158, 159, 160, 161, 162, 163, 164, 165,
166, 167, 168, 169, 170, 171, 172, 173, 174, 175, 176, 177, 178, 179, 180, 181, 182, 183, 184, 185,
186, 187, 188, 189, 190, 191, 199, 192, 193, 194, 195, 196, 197, 198, 200, 201, 202, 203, 204, 205,
206, 207, 208, 209, 210, 211, 212, 213, 214, 215, 216, 217, 218, 219, 220, 221, 222, 223, 224, 225,
226, 227, 228, 229, 230, 231, 232, 233, 234, 235

Stephen Message: 8, 9, 10, 11, 12, 13, 14, 15, 16, 17, 18, 19, 20, 21, 78, 79, 80, 81, 82, 83, 84, 85,
86, 87, 88, 89, 90, 91, 92, 93, 94, 95, 96, 97, 98, 99, 100, 101, 102, 103, 104, 105, 106, 107, 108,
109, 110, 111, 120, 121, 122, 123, 124, 125, 126, 127, 128, 129, 130, 131

Clive Byers: 54, 55, 56, 57, 63, 64, 65, 66, 67, 68, 69, 73

# Bill Oddie's
# BIRDS
## OF BRITAIN & IRELAND

NEW
HOLLAND

# CONTENTS

# CONTENTS

# INTRODUCTION

THIS BOOK WILL ENABLE YOU TO IDENTIFY THE BIRDS YOU ARE MOST LIKELY TO SEE IN BRITAIN AND IRELAND. I'm assuming that, generally, people see a bird, then look at the book and try to recognize it from the pictures. The first requirement therefore is that the illustrations are accurate, capturing not only the plumage, but also the shape and "feel" of the bird: what birdwatchers call the "jizz". Dave Daley, Clive Byers and Stephen Message are all masters of their craft, and the evidence is in these pages. I am confident that you will be able to identify most of what you see simply by recognizing the birds in the book. The only snag is that birds in the wild don't always pose and give you a great view. Moreover, there are a few species that do look very similar. The text will help you sort out these identification problems. I have tried to keep it short and to the point, stressing the key features to look for and in particular drawing attention to the possible "confusion species": birds that can be mistaken for one another. I have mentioned calls and songs only when they are distinctive or important to identifying the bird. We have *not* included lots of rarities, as they often confuse the issue.

Finally, a brief practical birdwatching tip: first, look at the bird (and listen) and take in as much as you can. Take notes or do a little drawing, if you like. Take particular note of the time of year (some birds are only summer or winter visitors), and the type of habitat the bird is in (many birds have a distinct preference). Note also the part of the country (some birds do not occur at all in certain regions), and what the bird is doing (behaviour is often distinctive and characteristic of certain species). Then, look it up in the book. You will find there is very little you won't be able to put a name to. If you really can't find it: maybe you've got a rarity!

## ACKNOWLEDGEMENTS

My thanks and gratitude to anyone who has written or illustrated a Field Guide in the past. The good ones were an inevitable source of inspiration, and the not-so-good ones helped me learn from their mistakes – I hope !

Also thanks to the many people I have had the pleasure (usually) of going birding with over the years. It is only by watching, studying and talking about birds "in the field" that we really get to know them. There is no substitute for experience.

Oh yes, and finally, thanks to the birds.

IF THE ILLUSTRATIONS ON THIS PAGE remind you of something you might see on a wall chart at a medical school, don't panic! Bird topography is indeed the avian equivalent of human anatomy.

Every area of feathers has an internationally agreed name. Some of them do sound rather scientific. However, learning these terms is not so difficult as it may seem at first. Many of them are pretty self-explanatory: for example, the bill, legs, rump and crown. Others sound more baffling, but in fact bird feathering follows a logical pattern and the topographical terms reflect this. For instance, the pattern on a bird's wing is more or less the same whatever the species and – once you understand the language, as it were - the names make sense: primaries (the first set of flight feathers), secondaries (second), tertials (third).

It is worth trying to get to know at least the basic terms as it does make it a lot easier if you are trying to write an accurate description or do a sketch of a bird you don't recognize. "Red median coverts, and white moustachial" is so much more specific than "red somewhere on the wing and white on the throat". So, next time a bird stays still long enough for you to study it, try comparing these diagrams with the feather areas on the real thing.

Having said all this, I have generally avoided the more daunting details in the descriptions in this book. Bird identification can be tricky and it is often a challenge – although a rather satisfying one – but, in fact, my first message is: above all, don't be put off.

It is definitely *not* so difficult as it may at first appear. Honestly!

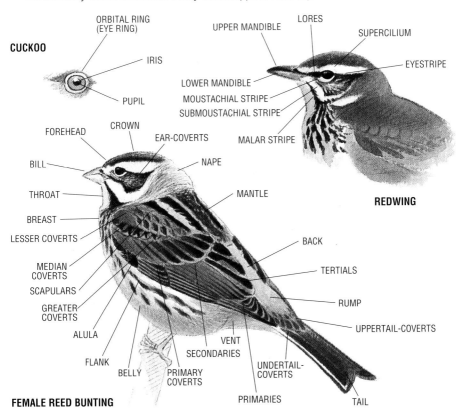

# RED-THROATED DIVER
### 52–58 CM, 21–23 IN

DISTINCTIVE IN BREEDING PLUMAGE in winter or juvenile plumage divers are all basically black (actually grey) above and white below. At a distance Red-throated can be confused with Great Crested Grebe, Cormorant or Shag, or "brownhead" Goosander or Merganser. Breeds on isolated lochs in Scotland. In winter, occurs on coasts round Britain, very occasionally on inland waters. At sea Red-throated is the commonest diver; inland the rarest. The "song" - only heard in breeding areas - is an eerie wailing.

Bill shape is key to identifying **non breeding plumage** divers (below). Note upturned bill (noticeable even in flight) and white face, isolating the eye. In **breeding plumage** (top) red throat can look almost black.

# BLACK-THROATED DIVER
### 58–68 CM, 23–27 IN

OCCURS ROUND COASTS (SEA AND ESTUARIES) out of the breeding season, and also occasionally on inland waters. Less common than Red-throat on sea, but more frequent inland (though still a rare bird). Rare breeder on lochs, only in Scotland. Non breeding and juvenile plumage is very similar to Red - throat. Most similar to Great Northern Diver, but is slightly rounder-headed, bill is thinner, white flank patch distinctive. Song – only heard in breeding areas – an eerie wail.

**Non breeding plumage** (top). Note straight bill, slightly thinner than Great Northern, conspicuous white flank patch. Distinctive **breeding plumage** (below). Black-throated is almost same size as Red-throated, but with a straight bill.

# GREAT NORTHERN DIVER

## 68–81 CM, 27–32 IN

BREEDING PLUMAGE RARELY SEEN – this species doesn't breed in Britain – except in spring in the northern isles or on Scottish coasts. At other times, occurs on the sea and estuaries all round the UK and occasionally on inland waters (sometimes even quite small ones). Small loose flocks may occur on coasts, but invariably solitary inland. In non breeding plumage the same "problems" as with the other two divers: i.e. confusable with Cormorants, and one another. Great Northern is the largest of the three divers. Note, in particular, the head shape: flat crown and square forehead. The bill is straight (unlike Red-throat) and a little thicker than Black-throat. It can appear quite pale (thus causing confusion with the very rare White-billed Diver. White-billed has slightly upturned look to the bill, which really is creamy white, including the upper edge). In flight, the Great Northern's large feet are conspicuous, sticking out behind. A final word on divers: non breeding birds *are* difficult, and even experts make mistakes!

**Non breeding plumage**. The largest diver. Most similar to Black-throated but note the flat head and thicker straight bill.

**Red-throated** (left). Note white face, visible eye and upturned bill. (Great Crested Grebe is smaller, with longer neck and more gangly in flight.) **Black-throated** (centre). Black cap and invisible eye. **Great Northern** (right). Large feet are conspicuous in flight. Body is bulky.

**Breeding plumage.** Occasionally seen in spring, but does not breed in Britain. (Cormorants and Shags look heavier than divers in flight and swim lower in the water.)

# LITTLE GREBE

### 27 CM, 10.5 IN

ALSO KNOWN AS DABCHICK. Fairly common and widespread, found all year round on inland waters, sometimes quite small ones. In winter, small flocks can occur on reservoirs and estuaries, but very rarely on the sea. Breeding plumage is distinctive, with rich chestnut neck and face and whitish puff-ball rear end. Youngsters are stripy and retain striped necks and heads for several weeks, even when fully grown. Non breeding plumage is much duller. Basically brownish above and whitish below, and the puff-ball look is often lost. This is when confusion is possible with the non breeding rare small grebes: Slavonian and Black-necked. In fact, they are both much cleaner black and white. They are also much rarer, and generally prefer coastal waters. General rule: on inland water, check that a distant small grebe isn't a Dabchick before considering the rarer ones. On estuaries and particularly on the sea a small grebe is more likely to be Slavonian or Black-necked. Song in the breeding season is a fast piping trill.

**Juvenile** (left) – the stripes fade as it gets older. Tiny chicks are sometimes carried on the parents' back. **Non breeding plumage** (below). They don't always have this puff-ball look, especially if they have been diving.

**Breeding plumage.** Dabchicks don't often stay as still as this! They hide in reeds and dive a lot, staying underwater for about 15 seconds.

# BLACK-NECKED GREBE

## 30 CM, 12 IN

ANOTHER VERY RARE BREEDING BIRD on just a few (usually secret or protected) inland waters such as lakes, large ponds and reservoirs, where it seeks cover in dense reedbeds or other vegetation. Picks insects off water surface. Tends to be very shy in the breeding season. Moves to coasts in winter. Slightly smaller than Slavonian Grebe, which it closely resembles. Breeding plumage distinctive: note black neck and pale yellow "ears". Non breeding plumage very similar to Slavonian Grebe and the same possible confusions occur (see Slavonian, page 14 and Little Grebe, page 10). Note that the bill is slightly upturned (straight on Slavonian), the blackish cap smudges down below the eye (clean above eye on Slavonian) and the white cheeks are more restricted (white almost meets on back of neck on Slavonian). Slightly domed top of head, compared with flatter head of Slavonian. The commoner of the two rarer small grebes on inland waters. Slavonian is commoner on the coasts; but neither is very numerous.

**Breeding plumage.** The tuft of yellow feathers behind the eye is fan-shaped. Americans call this species Eared Grebe – "golden-eared" would be more appropriate. A rare sight in Britain.

**Non breeding plumage.** Very similar to Slavonian Grebe, but note upturned bill, and black cap smudging below the eye, and rounder head shape created by steep forehead and high crown.

# SLAVONIAN GREBE
## 33 CM, 13 IN

BREEDS ONLY ON A FEW LOCHS IN SCOTLAND. You are only likely to see breeding plumage there, on sea lochs or estuaries in spring. Non breeding plumage is basically black above and white below. In winter (and autumn and early spring) may occur rarely on inland waters, and more commonly (but still not numerous) on estuaries or on the sea. Winter (non breeding) plumage is very similar to Black-necked Grebe. Note that Slavonian (Slav) has a straight bill, the black cap does not smudge below the eye, and white cheeks almost join at the back of the neck. Both rare small Grebes can be confused with winter plumage Dabchick, which can seem black and white, but are really shades of brown (see Little Grebe page 10). Also, young Coot are black and white, but only for a few weeks before they become all black. At a distance, some of the smaller female (or immature ) ducks can look a bit like small grebes (especially if they are asleep). See female Ruddy Duck and Smew.

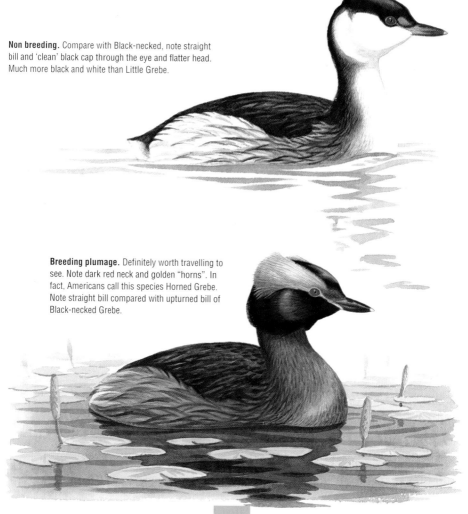

**Non breeding.** Compare with Black-necked, note straight bill and 'clean' black cap through the eye and flatter head. Much more black and white than Little Grebe.

**Breeding plumage.** Definitely worth travelling to see. Note dark red neck and golden "horns". In fact, Americans call this species Horned Grebe. Note straight bill compared with upturned bill of Black-necked Grebe.

# GREAT CRESTED GREBE

48 CM, 19 IN

WIDESPREAD AND COMMON, the Great Crested Grebe breeds on inland waters, but is scarcer in the north. It makes a nest of weeds near the water's edge, hidden among vegetation. Breeding plumage unmistakable, with conspicuous ear tufts and ruff, known as a "tippet". Chicks start stripy and retain head and neck stripes long after they are full grown. Non breeding (winter) plumage basically blackish (dark grey) above and white below. Confusion at a distance is possible with winter divers. Also – especially when asleep – with "brownhead" Goosander or Merganser. On the other hand, the white breast is very distinctive even at long distance. In winter, occurs on coasts (estuaries and sea). Confusion possible with Red-necked Grebe in non breeding plumage. Rule: Red-necked is a rare bird. (See Red-necked, page 14, for more.) It flies with neck extended and drooping, giving it a hump-backed appearance. Call: harsh barking and chattering, especially when in courtship display, which involves graceful necking and the "penguin dance", when both male and female almost seem to stand upright on the water.

**Juvenile** (at rear) retains its neck stripes long after it is fully grown.
**Non breeding plumage**. Great Cresteds occur on estuaries and on the sea in winter, so beware confusion with divers and other species.

**Breeding plumage.** Isn't it nice that such a spectacular bird is so common? The chicks leave the nest immediately after hatching and transfer to mother's back.

# RED-NECKED GREBE

## 33 CM, 13 IN

A RARE WINTER VISITOR, this species has tried to breed occasionally in Britain, especially northern Scotland, but its attempts are usually unsuccessful and its locations are kept secret. Breeding plumage is distinctive – red neck, white cheeks, black crown, yellowish beak – but like all the grebes it becomes much duller in non breeding plumage when it is very much like the Great Crested Grebe, but slightly smaller. It occurs mainly in winter months, rarely on inland waters, favouring gravel pits or lakes near the sea, or estuaries or offshore. Usually occurs as single birds. It is also seen on passage during the spring and autumn months. Told from Great Crested Grebe by slightly smaller and shorter stockier neck, and shorter bill, usually yellow-based. Duskier neck. Black cap down to the eye. Great Crested has white above the eye.

**Breeding plumage.** Unfortunately, this is a rare sight in Britain. Note red neck, white cheeks and, compared with Great Crested, absence of head ornaments.

**Non breeding plumage.** Most likely to be confused with non breeding Great Crested (see text). Never forget: this species is *much* rarer, even at sea in winter.

# FULMAR

47 CM, 18.5 IN

WIDESPREAD, BREEDING ON CLIFF LEDGES IN COLONIES, but more numerous in the north, Scotland and Northern Isles. Feeds at sea, mostly on fish. Population has grown rapidly in latter half of twentieth century. Superficially looks like a gull, but in fact belongs to the same family as albatrosses and shearwaters. At rest, grey above and white below, similar to many gulls, but note the distinctive "tube nose" on top of the bill, characteristic of its family. In flight over the sea, could be confused with a gull, but notice the wings lack any black at their tips. Often runs across the water surface to get airborne. Flies on very stiff wings, with much gliding, in typical shearwater style. It is, however, much greyer than any shearwater species, but – seen against the light – Fulmars can appear darker, and then confusion is possible. Good rule: if you think you are watching a shearwater gliding over the waves, are you sure it isn't a Fulmar?

The tube-nose filters out salt from sea water. Don't approach a nesting Fulmar – it will spit at you and cover you in foul-smelling oil!

Grey plumage rather like a gull, but note lack of black wing tips. The flight is stiff-winged, with a lot of gliding. Never seen inland – unless it's been seriously storm-driven.

# MANX SHEARWATER
## 35 CM, 14 IN
# SOOTY SHEARWATER
## 41 CM, 16 IN

**MANX** IS THE MOST NUMEROUS BRITISH SHEARWATER, but still only commonly seen near breeding areas: e.g. Welsh coastal islands, some northern and western isles and western Ireland. Unless you visit a colony at night with a torch, when the birds come to their burrows, you will only see shearwaters gliding low over the waves on stiff wings with intermittent flapping. Manxies are black above and clean white below. Possible confusions: Razorbills, Guillemots or Puffins, but they flap frantically all the time. Good seasonal rule: shearwaters are very unlikely in winter. Spring and especially late summer and autumn are the best times to see them on a sea watch. Calls, at the burrows: unearthly banshee-like grunts and wails. **Sooty** is the second commonest shearwater species in Britain, but is still a rare bird. Most likely to be seen offshore in late summer or autumn.

**Manx Shearwater.** Black above, white below, stiff-winged flight – the classic (and commonest) shearwater.

**Manx Shearwater.** As its name implies, it glides low over the waves, well out to sea.

**Sooty Shearwater.** Note the silvery underwings, which flash as it banks and glides. Slightly larger than Manxie and not really confusable with that species.

**Sooty Shearwater.** It really is sooty. Beware confusion with young Gannets, which are dark brown and do glide (Gannet is bigger and not such a fast flyer) also dark-phase skuas and even young gulls.

# STORM PETREL
### 15 CM, 6 IN
# LEACH'S PETREL
### 20 CM, 8 IN

**Storm Petrels** breed on remote islands in burrows – where they only come in at night – mainly off Scotland and western Ireland. You are most likely to see them off shore in the breeding areas, probably following in the wake of boats. They will almost certainly be in a flock, possibly quite a big one. The only really likely confusion (apart from some *very* rare petrels) is with **Leach's Petrel.** There are a few remote colonies in the northern isles off Scotland, but they are more or less unvisitable. Away from the nesting sites, it is in fact a rarer bird than Storm Petrel but you are more likely to see one because Leach's are fairly regularly driven closer to shore – or even inland – by bad weather, particularly in late autumn. A rule: if you see petrels over an estuary, or a single bird over a reservoir, it is almost certainly Leach's.

**Storm Petrel.** May occasionally be driven close to land – maybe into a harbour – after very rough weather. Flight is fluttery and it hovers and drops onto the water when feeding.

**Storm Petrel.** Tiny and fluttery, blacker than Leach's Petrel. Note white flash on underwing only. Never seen away from the sea.

**Leach's Petrel.** Pale patches on upperwing and more buoyant tern-like flight. It lacks Stormy's white underwing bar.

**Leach's Petrel.** Slightly bigger than Stormy, with longer more pointy wings, a less clear white rump and a slightly forked tail.

# GANNET

BREEDS IN COLONIES (OFTEN HUGE ONES) on cliffs and islands, mainly in the north, and Scotland and northern isles, with isolated colonies elsewhere. Adults on breeding grounds are unmistakable. Also occurs all round the coasts off shore among other seabirds. A line of Gannets is pretty distinctive, though they do bear some resemblance to a skein of geese (one of its other names is Solan Goose). Individual Gannets, however, can be quite puzzling, as they come in a variety of plumages, from the almost black very young birds, to the pure white with black wing tips of adults. If they are gliding on stiff wings they can look very like shearwaters or even albatrosses! (They have a 1.5 m (5 ft) wing span). If they soar high in the sky they may momentarily resemble skuas. Sitting on the water, they could even be mistaken for a diver! So, a rule when seawatching: if you see a large puzzling seabird, are you sure it's not a Gannet?

Gannets start life dark and get whiter as they get older. They take at least four years to mature. They can be confused with various other seabirds (see page 120).

Visit a Gannet colony for a noisy, smelly but unforgettable experience. They have a variety of interesting displays at the nest and when out fishing are the most spectacular divers.

# CORMORANT

FOUND ALL ROUND THE COASTS, breeding on cliffs and islands, sometimes in small colonies. Also increasingly numerous inland on reservoirs, rivers and even quite small ponds. There are even inland breeding colonies, usually in trees on islands on large lakes. May be seen perched high on trees, or on rafts, boats, islands, where it often adopts its famous wing-drying pose. Adults are generally black, with a white dot on the flank in full breeding plumage, and some may have almost all white heads. Young birds are browner and can be quite pale underneath. Possible confusions: they swim and dive, and at a distance could be mistaken for divers (see pages 8–9). Flocks often travel in V formation like geese. The only serious confusion is with Shag. Basic rule: inland, Cormorant is by far the commoner; a large flock on the coast is as – or more – likely to be Shags. Cormorants are common coastally but rarely in such concentrated numbers. Shag is in fact smaller with a steeper forehead (see Shag, page 20).

Some birds have white heads in **breeding plumage**. Cormorants are becoming increasingly common inland – to birdwatchers' delight and fishermen's alarm.

**Juvenile** (below left) is surprisingly pale below. This **adult** (below right) is not in the characteristic wing-drying pose for a change!

**Breeding plumage.** Note white patch on flank. Forehead less steep than on Shag.

# SHAG

Basically the Cormorant's smaller cousin. The plumage is very similar except in full breeding dress, when Shag has a quiff on its head, a greener sheen to the plumage, a yellow "gape" and green eye, and lacks any white on the face or the flanks. Juveniles are browner and paler below and generally have the pale area more extensive than on Cormorant. However, plumages can look pretty similar, in which case size and shape are the key. Shag is quite a lot smaller (but this is hard to judge unless they are side by side – which they sometimes are). The head shape is different: Shag has a rather steep forehead, smaller head and thinner bill. Shags are very unusual inland, whereas Cormorants are common. On the coast, Shags tend to form larger flocks, but of course not always. Swimming, similar to Cormorant, low in the water, but head shape and size are still discernible. Final comment: it's no shame to puzzle over isolated birds; experts also make mistakes.

In flight, Shag has faster wingbeats than Cormorant.

**Adult non-breeding** (far left) with **Juvenile** Shag (left) which is browner below than Cormorant.

**Breeding plumage**. Note quiff; steeper forehead than Cormorant.

# SIMILAR SPECIES: WINTER ON THE SEA

IN WINTER PLUMAGE, many species become basically black above and white below, or – in cold wintery light – can simply look black at a distance. Shape, size and "jizz" become all important.

Great Crested Grebe
Red-necked Grebe
Slavonian Grebe
Black-necked Grebe
Common Scoter (♀)
Eider (1st winter ♂)
Velvet Scoter (♀)
Velvet Scoter (♂)
Cormorant
Eider (♂)
Eider (♀)
Common Scoter (♂)
Long-tailed Ducks
Great Northern Diver
Shag
Guillemot
Black-throated Diver
Razorbill
Red-throated Diver
Black-necked Grebe
Great Crested Grebe
Black Guillemot
Red-necked Grebe
Slavonian Grebe

# BITTERN
## 75 CM, 30 IN

SADLY, BECOMING A VERY RARE BIRD. Only a few pairs now breed deep in the reedbeds in East Anglia and a few other protected marshes. Even there, they are not often seen. Your best bet is if one flies, which they occasionally do, though usually not for long, soon dropping back down out of sight. In fact, they are so rarely seen in flight that they are often puzzling: I have known them mistaken for birds of prey, day-flying owls or the rare Purple Heron! If you are very lucky you may see one "on the ground", most likely stalking through the reeds, or posing absolutely still, either waiting for fish or relying on its camouflage. As well as the few breeding sites, there are a number of fairly regular wintering marshes, possibly frequented by Continental rather than British birds. In fact, these are probably the best places to get a decent view, often from a hide. The call is an odd hollow "boom" like a distant foghorn.

Flights are usually brief before the bird disappears back into cover.

You'll be lucky to see a Bittern out in the open like this – but it's worth trying! If alarmed, the bird freezes to merge into the reeds.

# GREY HERON

## 90 CM, 35 IN

THE COMMON HERON IN BRITAIN, and found all over the region. Occurs all year round in a variety of habitats: marshes, ponds, lakes, rivers, canals, estuaries and even rocky sea shores. Hunts by stalking slowly through shallow water, or standing motionless and waiting for prey to come within reach. Usually nests in traditional colonies in trees. Juveniles lack some of the black neck markings of adults, but basically Grey Herons are pretty unmistakable. Nevertheless, they are sometimes reported as cranes. Cranes are in fact very rare and much bigger than even a Heron, and they fly with outstretched necks (Heron's neck is hunched). Flying Herons are sometimes a puzzle, especially if they are soaring high in the sky over the middle of a city. Firstly, remember that Herons really are not uncommon in urban areas. Secondly, they do soar and circle and are often mobbed by small birds, which presumably mistake them for large birds of prey, as indeed do people! Call sounds like "frarnk"; bill-clapping at nest.

In flight note head tucked back, legs extended behind. Wings broad and rounded. Slow, ponderous, wingbeats. **Juvenile** (below) is greyer than adult, without the head plumes.

Nests in traditional colonies, usually in tall trees. Builds huge nest of sticks, which is added to each year until it finally topples. Other bird species may nest in lower 'storeys'!

**Adult** birds have yellow bill, which turns pinkish in breeding season. Long black plumes on head. Several birds may gather together to rest at standing grounds.

# BEWICK'S SWAN
## 122 CM, 48 IN
# WHOOPER SWAN
## 152 CM, 60 IN

**BEWICK'S** IS THE SMALLER OF THE WILD SWANS. A winter visitor to Britain, and more numerous than Whoopers, particularly in the more southerly areas. There are places where both species occur and give you a chance to compare them (try Welney). Bewick's has a slightly shorter and thicker neck, and the bill is neater and the area of yellow smaller and rounder compared with Whooper's. Juveniles are grey and the yellow on the bill is replaced by pink. On a reasonable view these differences can be spotted when the birds are flying. The calls are slightly different: Bewick's is a shorter less echoing "bugle"; Whooper's a little stronger and eerier. **Whooper Swan** is about the same size as Mute Swan. Like Bewick's, has straight neck, yellow on bill and bugling call, and the juveniles are greyer, with pink bills. Compared with Bewick's, the shape of the yellow (or pink) is more pointed and extends further to the tip of the bill.

**Bewick's Swan adult** (right) and **juvenile** (below). As a general – but not infallible – rule, inland wild swans are more likely to be Bewick's.

**Whooper Swans**. Note extent of patterning on bill, extending further to tip, and shape of head compared with Bewick's. Whoopers have a few regular wintering grounds, generally more northerly than Bewick's.

24

# MUTE SWAN

## 152 CM, 60 IN

THE COMMON BRITISH SWAN. Some are barely wild and readily take food in parks and ponds; others prefer rather bleaker terrain on marshes and estuaries. The male (cob) has a larger bill knob than the female (pen). Juveniles start off grey and become whiter over the following couple of years. The bill also turns from grey to the adult black and orange. A swan is clearly a swan, unless seen at a distance asleep, in which case it could be mistaken for another large white bird, such as a Spoonbill or egret. There are also a few white (ex farmyard) geese around to confuse the issue! Distinguishing Mute Swan from the genuinely wild swans (Bewick's and Whooper) can be a little trickier. The Mute usually holds its neck in a graceful curve; wild swans' necks are straight. One basic fact to remember: wild swans are only winter visitors to Britain, and they generally favour regular wintering grounds.

In flight, Mute Swans' wings "whistle". Wild swans' wings are silent, but the birds rarely are; if you see them flying, you'll probably hear them bugling too.

Mute Swan **adult** (below left) and **juvenile.** Note black knob at base of adult's bill. Mute Swans are indeed mute (except for a few soft wheezy noises).

# GREYLAG GOOSE

## 76–89 CM, 30–35 IN

THE GREYLAG IS THE MOST WIDESPREAD OF OUR GEESE. Identifying the different species isn't easy. Calls are important. Greylags really do honk and squawk like their farmyard cousins. They belong to the group known as Grey geese. The important areas to note are the colour of legs and beaks, and any markings on the head, wings or belly. Greylags have large orange bills, pinkish legs, and a very pale chalky area on the upper forewing. A good rule is to get to know Greylag and then compare other grey geese with them. They occur all year round, but all the other species of grey geese are winter visitors, arriving in late September and October and leaving in March and April.

Many Greylags are not really wild birds, but originated on farms or collections and have "gone wild". They occur anywhere from park lakes to gravel pits, to remote marshes.

# PINK-FOOTED GOOSE

## 61–76 CM, 24–30 IN

OCCURS IN LARGE FLOCKS ON ITS FAVOURED WINTERING GROUNDS. The smallest and neatest of the grey geese and with a gentle expression, round-headed and short-necked. The neck and head are darker than the body. This is similar to Bean Goose but Beans are noticeably larger. Pinkfoot has pink on the bill, and also – of course – pink legs. The forewing is blueish-grey, but not as chalky as a Greylag. The call is a ringing "ung unk" and a higher pitched "wink wink wink". Most geese will sometimes fly in a V formation – they are famous for it – but don't assume that any distant V of large birds "must" be geese. Large gulls do it, also Cormorants and even Curlews.

In a flock of mixed grey geese, Pinkfeet are relatively easy to spot due to their small size, dark necks and heads, and faint pinkish tinge to their body colour.

ANOTHER GOOSE THAT OCCURS IN LARGE WINTERING FLOCKS. Two distinct races occur in Britain. Greenland Whitefronts winter in Ireland and Scotland; Russian birds visit Wales and southern England. The traditional sites are well known and the best places to see them. Greenland race birds have orange bills and orange legs. Birds of Russian race have pink bills and orange legs. The adults of both races have a white forehead (the "front"), and black belly markings. These markings are lacking on the juveniles, which are therefore more easily confused with other species. In fact, only juvenile Greenland Whitefront and Bean Goose share the same bill and leg colour. Bean has the darker neck, head and wings, and is much scarcer and more local, so the problem rarely arises. Also, fortunately, most geese occur in flocks where adults are also present. Whitefronts have a pale forewing and even paler line down the centre, but not as pale as either Pinkfoot or Greylag.

The call is higher pitched than the other grey geese, with a whinnying quality.

**Whitefront** (left) – dark upperwing; whinnying call. **Pinkfoot** (Centre) – small size, dark neck. **Greylag** (right) – large pale patch on upperwing . "Farmyard goose" call. Distant views, or small flying flocks, often puzzle even the experts and are sometimes recorded merely as "grey geese".

**Juvenile** (above) lacks the white forehead and black belly bars of the **adult** (foreground). These are Greenland birds – the European race has a pink bill.

# CANADA GOOSE
## 92–103 CM, 36–40 IN
# BARNACLE GOOSE
## 58–69 CM, 23–27 IN

THE **CANADA GOOSE** IS THE BEST KNOWN OF THE BRITISH GEESE, but is in fact native to North America. A common sight on just about any kind of water, particularly lakes and reservoirs, even in built up areas. If you see a small skein of geese flying inland, it's not a bad rule to start by assuming they are Canadas. Canada's call is a loud honking, rather like an old fashioned motor car klaxon. Genuine wild **Barnacles** are winter visitors in large numbers to a few favoured localities in Scotland and Ireland. Different populations breed in Greenland and Spitzbergen. On the wintering grounds, the flocks can be very large indeed – several thousands together. Smaller numbers may stop over at coastal locations in late autumn or spring but very rarely in the south of Britain. A single goose inland is almost certainly an escape! Barnacle's call is very like the distant barking of a pack of small dogs.

**Canada Goose**. Large size, with chinstrap and brown body. They are all over the place, present all year and breed freely! Rarely fly as high as genuine wild geese.

**Barnacle Goose**. Smaller and cleaner black and white than Canada. White face, grey body. Only in winter at regular sites. Favours closely grazed grassland, but roosts on saltmarshes or mudflats.

# BRENT GOOSE

## 56–61 CM, 22–24 IN

THE OTHER BRITISH BLACK GOOSE (with Barnacle). Winter visitor. Very much a coastal bird of estuaries, marshes and farmland near the sea. A small goose, black and white like a Barnacle, but lacking the white face. Two races occur in Britain: Light-bellied on the west coast and in Ireland, and Dark-bellied in the east and south. They are becoming increasingly numerous in some of their favoured locations, and each year a very small number linger well into late spring or even summer. Brents are very rare away from the coast, though small parties do occasionally occur on inland waters, most likely on migration in late autumn or early spring. The call is a rather growly "rronk"; and a flock sounds as if they are conversing in somewhat guttural tones! Single birds inland are likely to be escapes.

Canada Goose (left) – large, very rarely flies high, white chinstrap, honking call. Barnacle Goose (centre) – smallish, white face, barking call. Brent Goose (right) – small, dark head, growling call.

If you see a high-flying goose flock – even over town – that's the time to get excited! Look closely and listen for the calls.

Light-bellied Brent, with Dark-bellied race behind. A small, neat goose. Note Brent lacks the white face of Barnacle Goose. Feeds on coasts and estuaries.

A LARGE DUCK WITH GOOSE-LIKE SHAPE, AND WADDLY WALK. Present all year and breeds. Most common on the coast – estuaries and marshes – but also occurs – and even breeds – inland, particularly at gravel pits or reservoirs with shingly or muddy banks. The plumage is very striking and almost unmistakable. Only male Shoveler has similar colours – green head and orange flanks – but is very different in shape and habits (see Shoveler page 38). The male (Sheldrake) has the larger red knob on its beak. Its calls are a rhythmic whistling and a short grunt. Young birds lack the orange breast band and red bill, and can look rather odd, but are not really confusable with anything else. Breeds in burrows and rabbit-holes, often in sand dunes, and leads a large party of dark brown and white ducklings after hatching. Several broods sometimes combine into crêches. Adults gather in large flocks to moult after breeding. Gregarious, it is rarely seen singly.

➡ Often whistles in flight.

➡ **Juvenile** lacks orange breastband and green face. Generally "messier" but still the same, distinctive shape!

➡ **Female** almost identical to male. This duck swims buoyantly, but rarely far out to sea.

➡ **Male** has larger knob on top of the bill than the female does. Tends to feed by wading in shallow water and mud on the ebb-tide, sweeping for tiny snails in the soft mud.

# MANDARIN DUCK
## 43 CM, 17 IN

ANOTHER ONE THAT ISN'T A GENUINE WILD SPECIES IN BRITAIN, but has now been accepted on the official list. A native of China, it was originally "introduced" into ornamental wildfowl collections. There is now a small "feral" (semi-wild) population, largely in the southern counties. Favours lakes – often quite small ones – surrounded by trees and overhanging foliage. Mandarins often sit on banks in the shade, and are very hard to spot, which is a pity, since the male is among the world's most beautiful birds! However, like all drakes, it can look less impressive when it is in moult during the summer and early autumn. Female and young Mandarins are very sombre: soft grey plumage, with white chin and spectacle-like eye rings. Distinctive shape is clearly different from other female ducks, and, in any case, its habitat preference means it is rarely alongside any potential confusion species. Soft whistling call. Breeds in holes in trees.

This species is, in fact, very rarely seen in flight! Flight call is a sharp whistle.

**Female** – note the white spectacles. Confusable only with female Wood Duck – another wildfowl collection species.

**Male** – simply gorgeous in breeding plumage!

LARGELY A WINTER VISITOR, OCCURRING ON RESERVOIRS – particularly if they have grassy banks or farm fields nearby – and coastal marshes. Often seen in quite large flocks, feeding on pasture or mud, as well as swimming on the water. Male distinctive, with chestnut head and cream crown stripe, contrasting with pale pinky-grey body. In flight, white upper forewing patch is very obvious, and allows a flock to be identified even at considerable distance, for example, flying over the sea in late autumn. Female is less dull than most female ducks, having a richer chestnut tinge and bluish bill. Note the slightly domed head shape, which is clearly different from the other dabblers. In flight, female has a clean white belly, dark green speculum, and pale forewing, again making a distant flock distinctive. Eclipse males are like females but still have white forewings. The call is a descending whistle that can be heard for some way: one of the most atmospheric sounds of winter marshes and estuaries.

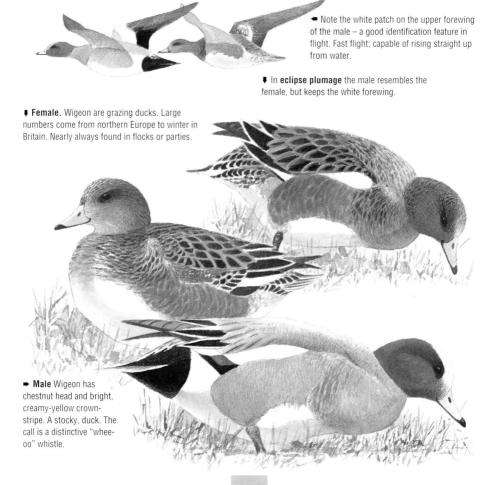

← Note the white patch on the upper forewing of the male – a good identification feature in flight. Fast flight; capable of rising straight up from water.

↓ In **eclipse plumage** the male resembles the female, but keeps the white forewing.

↓ **Female.** Wigeon are grazing ducks. Large numbers come from northern Europe to winter in Britain. Nearly always found in flocks or parties.

→ **Male** Wigeon has chestnut head and bright, creamy-yellow crown-stripe. A stocky, duck. The call is a distinctive "whee-oo" whistle.

# PINTAIL
## 66 CM, 26 IN (DRAKE); 56 CM, 22 IN (DUCK)

SIMILAR HABITAT PREFERENCES TO WIGEON AND – like that species – far commoner as a winter visitor to marshes and particularly estuaries, where it often feeds way out on the mud at low tide. The male is one of the most handsome ducks with its black "pin tail", chocolate head, and gleaming white breast, which stands out a mile away even on the gloomiest winter days. The female – despite its inevitable browny plumage – has a very distinctive shape: slender slim neck, all dark bill and a suggestion of the pin tail. A general note on the dabbling ducks: don't forget that all the males become like the females in eclipse plumage. Concentrate on the sizes and shapes – particularly the head shape – and speculum colour, and upper forewing patterns. Also, don't forget that although each species has its preferred habitats, they can turn up on more or less any bit of water on migration or during hard weather, and they all occasionally fly over the sea, and even land on it.

**Male** (left), **female** (right). Female's slim neck, suggestion of pin tail stand out even in flight, along with a rather plain upperwing and dark dull speculum (the patch on the rear inner wing).

**Female** (right). Pintails are dabbling ducks like Mallard and Teal, and often occur with Wigeon, but note longer neck and more slender appearance.

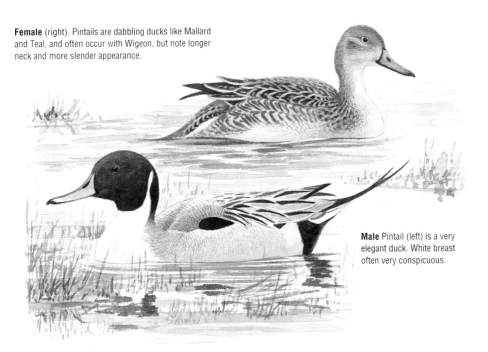

**Male** Pintail (left) is a very elegant duck. White breast often very conspicuous.

# GADWALL

51 CM, 20 IN

NOT A VERY NUMEROUS SPECIES but seems to be increasing and is present throughout the year. Occurs mainly on inland waters and only very occasionally coastal marshes or estuaries. Male is distinctive: soft grey with black stern. Note the white speculum with chestnut and black edges. Female is very like Mallard but just a little smaller. The white speculum is the best feature and is often visible even before the bird flaps its wing. A rare breeding bird, and even in winter doesn't often form large flocks. The white speculum allows identification of even distant flying birds, but note that some of the diving ducks also show a similar marking, for example female Goldeneye (see page 50). A general note – although male ducks in eclipse are difficult to distinguish from the females, they retain the characteristic speculum colour.

**Female** (left), **male** (right). Flight is rapid, rather like Wigeon's. White speculum and cleaner white belly than Mallard.

**Female** Gadwall (right) very like female Mallard, but note white speculum often visible "peeping" out. Orange-yellow legs visible when upends.

**Male** Gadwall (left) rather dull but distinctive. Note grey bill. Female's is horn-coloured with orange sides. A dabbling duck, like Mallard and Teal.

# MALLARD

## 58 CM, 23 IN

THE COMMON WILD DUCK IN BRITAIN and many other parts of the world. Widespread breeder on all watery places from tiny ponds to coastal areas, sometimes even some way away from water. Male is familiar to most of us. Female is dull speckly brown, like many ducks. A good rule though: get to know your female Mallard and compare other species with it. Note head shape and size. Farmyard ducks are descended from the Mallard, and wild birds, especially in towns, often have patches of white in their plumage or may be pale in colour. The Mallard is a large duck, with a fairly large bill. Note also the purple speculum – the shiny patch on the wing. The call is the familiar quack. General note: ducks fall into a few convenient groups. On inland waters, dabbling ducks – which feed by dipping their beaks beneath the surface or upending – and diving ducks – which do just that. They dive and swim under the water. Mallard is the archetypal dabbling duck, and the one to act as your basic comparison for all other ducks.

The Mallard is a powerful, strong flyer, and will rise straight from the water. Note purple speculum.

**Female** Mallard (left) has greenish bill; male's is yellow. Feet are bright orange-red. Compare shape with other dabbling ducks, especially Shoveler.

The **male** Mallard (above) is very handsome – note the curly tail! Mallards are fairly catholic in their diet and feed by upending or taking seeds from the water surface.

35 CM, 14 IN

THE SMALLEST DABBLING DUCK. Most likely to be seen in winter on large lakes – often hiding in cover at the edges – or on marshes and estuaries, where flocks may feed out in the open on the mud or on nearby grazing meadows. Always seem to be nervous and rarely allow close approach. Becomes even harder to see during the breeding season. Male is unmistakable: chestnut head with green eyepatch and striking creamy yellow undertail. The white flash along the side is conspicuous even at very long range. Female is typical brown mottled duck. Identify by small size and green speculum. Most similar to female Garganey (see page 37), Garganey has stripier face and is summer visitor only. Call is an odd short "peep peep", quite unlike a quack. Flocks of Teal fly very fast and low, and can be mistaken for waders at a distance over estuaries or marshes, or even over the sea during migration periods.

**Male** (left), **female** (right). Small size and green speculum. Teal fly very fast and low, often in tight flocks. Rise straight up from the water.

**Female**. Teal really are small – this is very noticeable when they are feeding alongside other species. Both male and female have grey bill.

**Male**. White flash on flanks is visible at long range. Creamy-yellow undertail is also a useful feature.

# GARGANEY

38 CM, 15 IN

THE SUMMER TEAL. A dabbling duck that is a summer visitor to Britain, more commonly to the southern half of the country. It arrives in March and leaves by the end of September (rarely October). Usually seen in singles or pairs, and very occasionally small parties, but never in flocks like Teal. Much prefers secluded small lakes or fresh marshes, with reeds and ditches, and usually keeps to cover at the edges. The male is very distinctive, with a purplish head and vivid white eye brow, and shows pale blue shoulders when it flies. Female is very like female Teal but look for the paler stripes above and below the eye and paler forewing in flight. Flies fast but without the sharp twists and turns of Teal. Like all species of ducks, juveniles – and males in eclipse plumage – resemble females, but the males retain a much paler forewing. Not particularly common.

**Male** (far left) and **female**. Compare with Teal. Note pale forewing – less bright on female, but still paler than Teal. Flight is rapid, but not so wader-like as the flight of the Teal.

**Female.** Notice stripier face pattern than female Teal.

**Male.** The vivid white eyebrow may be all you see when the bird is swimming among reeds and lilies.

# SHOVELER

LIKE MOST OF THE BRITISH BREEDING DUCKS, a bird that is much easier to see in winter, when small flocks occur on inland waters and coastal wetlands. The male is very distinctive, with green head, orange flanks, and bright white breast, which is easily seen even at long distance. In flight, it has a bluish forewing. Female and juvenile: typically brown – like Mallard or Teal – but note the obvious large bill and the distinctive feeding method: low in the water, dipping the head from side to side. Orange feet very conspicuous. Eclipse male can look a little like a Garganey, as it has a bluer caste to the head and whitish crescent in front of the eye, and bluish wing patches; but note the bill shape and larger size. Feeding flocks sometimes swim so close together it's hard to count them! Often, when food is plentiful, they seem to feed in co-operation, individual birds revolving slowly on their own axis in the water as they constantly nibble just beneath the water surface.

➡ **Male** and **female** (far right). The blue forewing is the only colour on the otherwise drab female. Note the exceptionally large bill. Flies readily and well, but is a poor walker.

◄ **Female.** Like other duck species, the female alone incubates the eggs. Shovelers usually nest on dry ground not far from water.

➡ **Eclipse male** in late summer/autumn. Shovelers tilt forward to feed, swimming low in water. Do not up-end so readily as other dabbling ducks, but can dive.

◄ **Male.** The white breast is very conspicuous even at long distance. The huge bill is edged with a tiny fringe that filters seeds and other food from the water.

# POCHARD

ONE OF THE COMMONEST OF THE DIVING DUCKS. Present throughout the year. Large flocks occur in winter, although it is scarcer as a breeding species. Almost exclusively on inland waters, from small lakes to huge reservoirs. May occur on rivers or even estuaries during hard weather. Male is distinctive: black at both ends, pale grey in the middle, with striking orangey head. Female – as ever! – generally dull plumage. Often seen in company with Tufted Ducks. Female Pochard has greyer caste than female Tufted, with paler areas on face, including greyish spectacles. Note the Pochard's characteristic head shape: steep sloping forehead. Tufted's head shape is rounder. In flight, Pochard has rather uniform upperwing , lacking a vivid wing stripe. Pochard tend to feed at night, so you are more likely to see them snoozing by day, with bill tucked back under a wing, often gathered together in rafts bobbing gently on the water. (See also Ferruginous Duck, page 225)

**Males** in flight. Diving duck "skitter" across the water surface before taking off, and, when disturbed, will move out onto open water rather than take to the air.

**Female.** Greyer than female Tufted. Note pale patch on face and "spectacles". Pochard usually dive for food – mostly plant material – but will up-end.

**Male.** Note the typical posture – Pochard look rounded. Distinctive head shape with sloping forehead. Pochard often roost on water by day.

# RUDDY DUCK
## 41 CM, 16 IN

REALLY A NORTH AMERICAN SPECIES, introduced to Britain in wildfowl collections, but has now established a wild population that has increased and spread from its stronghold in the Midlands – despite attempts to control it! Possibly their ability to have two broods of ducklings a year has contributed to their population explosion. Large flocks occur in winter on some southern reservoirs. Much more secretive during the breeding season, dives frequently and hides in reeds and overhanging foliage. Small and dumpy with sticking up "stiff tail". Male: very striking in breeding plumage, with bronzed body, gleaming white cheek and blue bill (fades in winter ). Female and juvenile: greyish brown with pale face, with stripe across the cheek. The white-cheeked look is a little like female Common Scoter or Long-tailed Duck – both of which can occur on inland waters – or brownhead Smew, especially if the bird is distant or asleep. Note the Ruddy's distinctive dumpy stiff-tail shape. Very rarely seen in flight – but they must fly to spread so successfully!

A rare sight – Ruddy Duck in flight.

**Females** and **juveniles** are very similar. Both male and female share pale-faced look with some other species – compare Smew, Common Scoter and Long-tailed Duck.

**Male** is unmistakable in breeding plumage. Has a variety of displays during courtship, including a wonderful "bobbing" display, and one in which it creates a surge of bubbles in front of it.

# EIDER

58 CM, 23 IN

A DUCK OF THE SEA AND ROCKY COASTAL AREAS, far commoner in the north and in Scotland and Ireland, where it also breeds. Large flocks form in autumn and winter, which also consist of non breeding birds. It is much scarcer in the south of Britain – most likely offshore in autumn or winter – and very rare indeed on inland waters. Male is unmistakable in breeding plumage. However, young and eclipse males can look very blotchy and are very variable. Some look almost all dark, with a few white patches on the wings, whereas others have white breasts. Females are brown all over. Note the characteristic wedge-shaped head with long triangular bill. If you see any duck on the sea with this shape – even if the plumage is puzzling – it is probably an Eider. The only species that has a similar shape is Velvet Scoter, which is much rarer (see Velvet Scoter, page 47). Call of male Eider is a surprised sounding cooing: "oo oo oo".

**Male** (far left) and **female.** The triangular head is noticeable even in flight. Has a strong, direct flight. usually low over water. Large numbers winter off British coasts.

**Young males** (right) often show this white-breasted look, but can have much messier patterns. The *shape* is distinctive. **Adult male** at foot of page.

**Female** (below). Note triangular head-shape; this is a useful distinguishing feature from other female ducks.

# TUFTED DUCK
## 43 CM, 17 IN

The commonest diving duck on inland waters, occurring in large winter flocks, but scarcer as a breeding bird. Often with Pochard. Male: clean black and white. Confusion only really possible with Scaup (page 43), which rarely occurs inland. Note grey back of male Scaup, slightly larger size, and complete lack of crest or tuft on the head. Female Tufted compared with Pochard: darker brown, less grey plumage, and rounder forehead, giving quite different head shape. Many female Tufteds have a whitish area round the base of the bill, which makes them confusable with female Scaup. Female Scaup is larger, often has pale patches on the cheek, and the white area round the bill base is larger and clearer. Also remember that Scaup really is a rare bird inland, and is also a winter visitor. Nevertheless, even experts often puzzle over blotchy female Tufteds. Also note that some female Tufteds have white under the tail and resemble the rare Ferruginous Duck (see page 225). Ferruginous has a Pochard-shaped head, with steep forehead, and generally more gingery tinge to the plumage.

**Female** (right) and **male.** In flight, Tufted shows a bright white wing bar, which stands out even at a distance.

**Female** has rounder head shape than female Pochard. The white on the head is variable and it can often show white undertail, although this particular bird doesn't.

**Male.** The "tufted" bit is on the back of the male's head. Compare with Scaup, but remember that Scaup is rarely found inland.

# SCAUP
## 48 CM, 19 IN

MAINLY A WINTER VISITOR TO BRITAIN, and prefers the sea or inlets and estuaries, particularly in the north and in Scotland and Ireland. Often occurs in large flocks, which may extend into a long line of birds. It can occur on inland waters – especially in migration periods or during hard weather – but usually only in very small numbers. If you think you see a Scaup inland, look hard to make sure it isn't a Tufted or a hybrid. Male is very similar to Tufted but with a grey (not black) back and no head crest. At distance in poor light, Pochard can look similarly dark at both ends, but in fact Pochard's head is chestnut, and the head shape is different. Female Scaup is like a rather bulky female Tufted, but with larger cleaner area of white at the base of the bill, often with pale blotches on the face, and a slightly sandier overall plumage tinge. In flight, Scaup also has a white wing bar, similar to Tufted Duck.

**Male** (left) and **female.** Similar flight pattern to Tufted Duck.

**Female.** Note large white area at base of bill and pale blotches on cheeks compared with female Tufted Duck.

**Male.** Note pale back compared with male Tufted. Scaup are mainly sea ducks, feeding largely on molluscs.

# LONG-TAILED DUCK

DRAKE 53 CM, 21 IN; DUCK 41 CM, 16 IN

A SEA DUCK BUT ONE THAT PREFERS SHELTERED BAYS AND ESTUARIES. It also occurs occasionally – usually only ones or twos – on inland waters, particularly gravel pits. A winter visitor. You are only likely to see large numbers in the north and in Scotland and the Northern Isles (Shetland and Orkney). The male's complicated black (actually dark brown ) and white patterns are almost reversed from non breeding to breeding plumage. The birds become darker as the spring progresses. Adult males have the wonderful long tail.

Females and immatures are always duller, basically brownish above, white below, with white brown-blotched faces. It's hard to describe, and in fact the plumage varies between individuals. Birds like this occurring inland are often a bit of puzzle, somewhat resembling female Ruddy Duck, Common Scoter or even Pochard. Long-tailed is rare inland, so if you think you've got one, make sure to eliminate other confusion species. Dives continually. On sunny days, especially in spring, you may hear the cooing display call (like a small Eider).

← **Male** (far left) and **female.** Unmarked, "solid" dark wings contrast with the pale body and head plumage, making for a very distinctive pattern.

→ **Male. Breeding plumage.** Only likely in late spring in the north.

↓ **Non breeding male.** Arguably prettier than the breeding plumage.

↑ **Female.** Young birds look basically like females but are variable and can be a bit of a puzzle (see text). Remember that Long-tailed is rare inland.

44

# SMEW
## 41 CM, 16 IN

WINTER VISITOR IN SMALL NUMBERS TO INLAND WATERS, particularly gravel pits. Also found on estuaries and inlets. Has a few favourite regular sites, and is more common some winters than others, particularly if it is cold on the continent. The Smew is the smallest of the sawbills (which have serrated beaks for gripping fish). The male is exquisite – unmistakable – brilliant white, with black "cracks" and eye patch. Female and juvenile are grey, with chestnut crown, and white cheeks. Ruddy Duck and female Common Scoter also have the white-cheeked look, but are different shapes, and the crown is not chestnut. Brownhead Goldeneye, with which Smew often occurs, has similar habits – constantly diving – and basically similar colours, but lacks the white cheeks. Brownhead Smew are considerably more numerous than the lovely males in breeding plumage – a pity! A shy and almost silent bird, it flies fast and is an expert diver.

**Female** and **male** (far right). Only likely to be seen "skittering" across the water when disturbed. Adult male looks more pied in flight than when on water.

**Female** or **juvenile** – known as brownheads or redheads – arguably "chestnut-head" would be most appropriate. Some other species have this white-faced look (see text).

**Male.** Small, neat and very pretty. Sadly, also pretty scarce in Britain, which provides wintering grounds for more female and juvenile birds.

# COMMON SCOTER

48 CM, 19 IN

BY FAR THE COMMONER OF THE TWO SCOTERS. A sea duck which occurs in large flocks, mainly in winter, but also throughout the year in northern areas and Scotland. A rare breeder on a few remote Scottish and Irish lochs. Most likely to be seen on the sea or flying by on a seawatch. Also a surprisingly frequent visitor to large inland reservoirs, even sometimes during summer months. The male is all black, with yellow on the beak. Confusable only with Velvet Scoter. Common has no white on the wing. Female Common is dark brown with pale cheek (that can look almost white). A female – especially on an inland reservoir – can be confused with female Ruddy Duck, Smew or Red Crested Pochard, all of which have the pale-cheeked look. The Scoter is in fact considerably chunkier than all of them. In flight, Scoter males look all black and females more or less all brown: no wing markings on either.

**Males** are the only genuinely all black duck in flight – but other species and distant flocks of ducks can look black in poor light or in silhouette.

**Female.** Several other species have this pale-faced look (see text and compare Ruddy Duck, Smew, Red Crested Pochard).

**Male.** Only Velvet Scoter is as black but Common has no white on face or wings.

46

# VELVET SCOTER

56 CM, 22 IN

OCCURS ONLY VERY RARELY INLAND. You are most likely to see it in winter with other sea ducks (especially Common Scoter) or flying past on a seawatch. In flight, both male and female show a bright white speculum on the upperwing , which immediately separates them from Common Scoter or Eider; but note that female Goldeneye also has a white speculum and may fly by on a seawatch. Female Goldeneye is smaller, with paler body and chocolate brown head – points noticeable even in distant flight. Male Velvet Scoter is similar shape and size to Eider, but has yellow on the beak and small white patch under the eye, and is otherwise black. Female and juvenile are dark brown with whitish blotches on the face. The main problem is often that they dive constantly, way out on rough seas, and it's hard to get a decent view, even with a telescope. It is always worth sorting through any flock of Common Scoters for the occasional Velvet.

In flight, both male and female look black or very dark, but with vivid white speculum.

**Female.** "Eider"-shaped head but sooty plumage. **Juvenile** looks very similar. Both male and female often show the white speculum even when swimming on the water.

**Male.** Only Common Scoter is as black. If white speculum is not visible, you may have to wait for Velvet to flap its wings.

# RED-BREASTED MERGANSER

## 58 CM, 23 IN

PRESENT THROUGHOUT THE YEAR, the Red-breasted Merganser is very similar to the Goosander. Although mainly a winter visitor, it breeds in remote mountainous and moorland areas in small numbers, nesting on the ground. However – when not breeding – it much prefers coastal habitats – bays and estuaries – where Goosander is much less likely. Smaller than Goosander. Male Merganser is much less "clean" than Goosander. Note brown breast and greyer flanks. Brown breast band may also be distinguishing feature in flight. Theoretically male Mergansers have similar colours to a male Mallard, but confusion isn't very likely. "Mergs" dive a lot and have shaggy crest and scarlet saw-bill. Female and juvenile are very like Goosander, but note wispier crest, less clear-cut white chin and overall scrawnier look, and preference for salt water. Merganser is very rare inland. In flight, "brownheads" even more similar to Goosander; hopefully, there will be males with them! Distant, constantly diving Mergsansers can be mistaken for Divers or Cormorant/Shag.

**Female** and **male** (far right). Note large white patches on upperwing – much more than a mere speculum! Note brown breast band on male.

**Female** or **young birds** are known as "brownheads": compared with very similar Goosanders, they are more diffuse between brown head and whitish breast, and spikier crest.

**Male.** Wonderfully scruffy! Compare with clean-cut Goosander.

# GOOSANDER

66 CM, 26 IN

THE LARGEST SAWBILL. MAINLY A WINTER VISITOR but some breed in remote areas mainly in northern Britain. Like the Red-breasted Merganser, it feeds largely on fish; unlike Mergansers, it nests in tree holes or among rocks. Mainly winters on large reservoirs, but will also visit rivers and estuaries. Male: vivid white, with dark green head (looks black at a distance), and scarlet bill. Female and juvenile: grey body, brown head, with slight shaggy crest, very similar to "brownhead " Merganser (see opposite page). Goosander has less crest, cleaner white chin and slightly stockier build. Like other sawbills, patters along water surface before getting air-borne. Remember that Goosander is by far the commoner species on inland waters; Mergansers prefer coastal areas. In flight, female Goosanders have whitish broken speculum like Smew, but the patch is much larger. At a distance and in poor light, Goosanders and Mergansers can be confused with divers or Cormorants/Shags, so look carefully at the shape and plumage colours.

Female (left) has less white on wing than female Merganser. Male (far left) has more white on wing – and anywhere else – than Merganser.

Female. Compare with Merganser – note clean line between brown head and white breast.

Male. Dazzlingly white, very conspicuous even at long distance.

# GOLDENEYE
## 46 CM, 18 IN

DIVING DUCK. A WINTER VISITOR. One of the few species that is almost equally at home at the coast or on inland waters. Rarely occurs in large numbers – fifty in one place would be a lot – but is quite widespread. Just a few breed – in trees – mainly in remote parts of Scotland. Male: very conspicuous even at long range. Brilliant white and black (actually the head is dark glossy green but often looks black). Female and juvenile: grey body, brown head. Young males look like females but with more white in the wing.

In flight, the **male** (left) has very large white wing patch. **Female** (far left) has smaller white speculum on upperwing, similar to Velvet Scoter. The scoter is larger and darker.

**Female.** Slightly similar to brownhead Smew or female Ruddy Duck, but Goldeneye has wholly dark chocolate-brown head, and is confusable mainly because they keep diving and giving only brief views!

**Male.** Note large head with noticeable peaked forehead. White face-spot conspicuous even from a distance.

LAST WORDS ON DUCK IDENTIFICATION: males are generally pretty easy. Anything puzzling is likely to be a female or young bird. If the plumage doesn't quite fit the book it may well be a male in eclipse (moult), particularly in late summer and early autumn. Despite habitat preferences, birds can occur in the "wrong" places (e.g. sea ducks inland, and inland ducks offshore). If you are really baffled: it might be a hybrid or an escape.

Male Common Scoter

Male Long-tailed Duck.

Female Long-tailed Duck

Female Common Scoter

ESPECIALLY IN AUTUMN AND WINTER, a large number of otherwise distinctive species can look rather drab. Many of them are basically dark grey above, with whitish faces. This page shows a selection for direct comparison. Compare, for example, Common Scoter with Ruddy Duck and Smew; and the Slavonian Grebe with juvenile Coot and Little Grebe; and the juvenile Moorhen with the Water Rail. As with other groups, habitat preferences can be a useful guide – the Long-tailed Duck, for example, is rare inland.

Slavonian Grebe

"Brownhead" Smew

Female Ruddy Duck

Female Teal

Great Crested Grebe (winter plumage)

Little Grebe (winter plumage)

Juvenile Coot

Juvenile Moorhen

Water Rail

ALL THE SPECIES ON THIS PAGE ARE DIVING DUCKS. The habitat will often help identify them. Are they on the sea, a large stretch of inland water, or a smaller reedy pool? On the opposite page are the female dabbling ducks, which do look very similar to each other – basically mottled brown. However, they all have their own distinctive shapes, plumage features, as well as characteristic ways of feeding and flying. Use the familiar Mallard for a reference point and comparison. Nearby male ducks will often enable you to work out what the females are, but the most difficult time of year is in late summer when most males are in eclipse plumage and resemble the females! As with marine species, ducks and other waterbirds can appear simply as silhouettes, so the more you know about jizz the better! See also the main species pages for more information.

Female Goldeneye and juveniles often referred to as "brownheads". May occur on any water in winter. Tufted and Pochard usually on inland waters. Scaup usually in winter and in an estuary or at sea. Note that Ring-necked Duck is very rare!

Tufted Duck

Goldeneye

Scaup

Pochard

Ring-necked Duck

Ruddy Duck

Goosander

Smew

Red-breasted Merganser

Goosander, Merganser and Smew are all known as "redheads" or "brownheads" in female or juvenile plumage. Merganser has shaggier crest, less clear outline than Goosander. Smew occurs inland in winter. Ruddy Duck occurs only inland and in winter in flocks on large lakes.

Velvet Scoter, Common Scoter, Long-tailed Duck and Eider occur mainly on the sea and are also diving ducks. The other birds on this page are all dabblers.

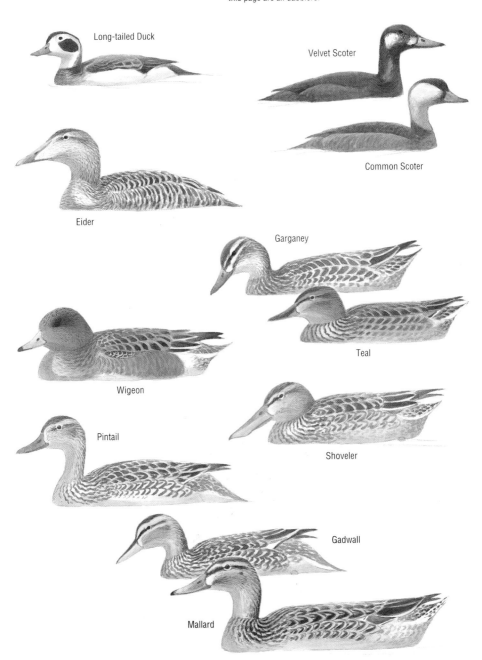

Long-tailed Duck

Velvet Scoter

Common Scoter

Eider

Garganey

Teal

Wigeon

Pintail

Shoveler

Gadwall

Mallard

# RED KITE

A LARGE GRACEFUL RAPTOR, with the looks of a harrier and the habits of a Buzzard! Genuinely British Red Kites are restricted to Wales, where the breeding population seems to be very healthy and slightly increasing. Scandinavian birds have also been introduced to English counties and are doing well. These may have noticeable wing tags on them. Red Kite has long slim wings, a deeply forked tail and a foxy red tinge to the plumage, with whitish wing patches. At a distance, the forked tail may not be easy to see, in which case the flight style is the best feature to distinguish Red Kites from Buzzards, which are likely to be in the same area. Once seen, not easily forgotten! In the breeding season, Kites favour wooded valleys, where they can be very hard to spot, but there is a large winter roost in Wales, where up to a hundred birds have been seen together. Well worth a visit.

All ages and both sexes look much the same – unusual for a raptor, and something of a relief as it makes for fewer identification problems! Note forked tail and large pale wrist patches of these two in flight. The Red Kite glides on flat wings (Buzzards in a 'V'), often twists its tail like a rudder, rocking from side to side.

Like so many birds of prey, kites are easier to identify in flight than when perched.

# MARSH HARRIER
## 48–56 CM, 19–22 IN

HARRIERS ARE LARGE BIRDS OF PREY, AS BIG AS BUZZARDS, but with longer narrower wings and longer tails, usually held closed. They typically fly low over reedbeds or farmland, with a flap and glide style, wings held in a shallow 'V', and often gently swaying from side to side, sometimes hovering and dropping onto invisible prey. Once seen, this flight style is not difficult to recognize. So, once you feel sure it is a Harrier you are looking at, you have three species to choose from. Marsh Harrier is the most likely, though it is still not numerous and is restricted as a breeding bird to East Anglia. It is becoming more widespread. Prefers habitats that contain reedbeds or at least some wet areas. The bulkiest of the British species. Noticeably a little heavier and broader winged in flight. Like the other harriers, Marsh doesn't often soar up high and circle on the thermals – but it can! In which case, note the long narrow winged look compared with Buzzard.

**Female** and **juveniles** (left and above) are completely chocolate brown, except for variable creamy markings on the crown and shoulders. No white rump.

**Male** (above and right). Complicated pattern of pale grey, black and brown – but there's nothing quite like it. Not so clean cut as Montagu's or Hen males.

**Male.** Neither sex has the white rump – "ring tail" – that distinguish Montagu's or Hen Harrier females.

# HEN HARRIER

43–51 CM, 17–20 IN

SLIGHTLY SMALLER THAN MARSH HARRIER (or Buzzard), with correspondingly slimmer build and narrower wings. The flight style is typically harrier-like (see Marsh) but Hen Harriers are less addicted to watery habitats. They breed (in small numbers) on treeless moorlands (particularly where there are grouse (which has made them the victim of illegal poisoning or shooting). The male is ghostly pale grey, with black dipped-in-ink wing tips. Even cleaner cut than male Montagu's (see page 57). Female and young birds are known as "ringtails", because of the white upper tail band (rump), the only white area on the otherwise largely brown plumage. Ringtail Hen is very difficult to separate from Montagu's in similar plumage. It has a slightly heavier build, but this is hard to judge without experience. The really fine points of this tricky identification are covered in specialist books. Meanwhile, it's not a bad rule that birds seen in winter are almost certainly Hen Harrier, and especially if they are in a loose gathering at a roost.

Juveniles and females (left) are known as "ring-tails" but this one is hiding this feature (see Montagu's Harrier).

Male (right). Cleaner and more ghostly than male Montagu's. Also, the wing tips are black.

Male (right) and female (below right). Female can be difficult to tell from female "Monty's" but remember that Hen Harrier is the commoner of the two.

# MONTAGU'S HARRIER
### 41–46 CM, 16–18 IN

VERY LIKE HEN HARRIER, BUT A SUMMER VISITOR ONLY, arriving April and leaving by late September or early October. A scarce and decreasing breeder at a few well protected sites, mainly in eastern England. Just a little slimmer and more graceful than Hen Harrier – sometimes likened to a large falcon – but it is hard to judge with a single bird. Males basically grey with black wing tips; also have thin dark lines running down the upperwing and light barring on the tail, and this makes them look less "clean" than Hen Harrier. Ringtails are very similar to Hen but the slimmer build may catch your eye, and the white rump may be narrower and therefore less vivid than on Hen. If seen well, perched – which frankly isn't often with harriers! – young Montagu's have almost – or entirely – unstreaked apricot coloured breasts and bellies. Like Marsh Harrier, neither Hen nor Montagu's are often seen soaring, but it can and does happen, especially if the birds are migrating.

**Female** and **juveniles** (below right) known as "ringtails" because of conspicuous white upper tail band. **Male** (below) less clean-cut wing pattern than Hen, with black bars along inner wing.

**Male** (left, above left) – compare less clean-cut appearance with male Hen Harrier (opposite). Montagu's are summer visitors to Britain and only a few pairs breed.

THE SECOND COMMONEST SMALL RAPTOR IN BRITAIN, often confused with the commonest: the Kestrel. Sparrowhawks in fact belong to a different group – the accipiters – whereas Kestrel is a falcon. Falcons have slender, pointed wings – as does Kestrel – but Sparrowhawk's wing tips are more rounded. The flight style of a Sparrowhawk is quite distinctive: a shallow flap and glide, that is hard to describe but once seen is clearly different from Kestrel. Both species can soar and circle, in which case, the wing shape is the best point to note, if you can't see plumage details (which is often the case with flying birds of prey). One perfectly safe rule though: Sparrowhawks do *not* hover. Also Sparrowhawks generally hunt in wooded habitats, including gardens, where they glide low among foliage in pursuit of small birds. It used to be a fairly safe rule that any small raptor over a town would be a Kestrel, but Sparrowhawks are increasing and moving into urban areas. The commonest call is a loud "kek kek kek".

Typical Sparrowhawk flight is a shallow flap and glide. Sparrowhawks do not hover. They hug hedges and boundaries when hunting, preying mostly on small birds.

Both **male** (above) and female have horizontal bars on their under bodies (Kestrel's streaks are vertical). The **male** is grey above, but the female and youngsters brown.

**Females** (right) can be much bigger than males, and the biggest may be mistaken for the rare Goshawk (see opposite).

# GOSHAWK

### 48–61 CM, 19–24 IN

VERY MUCH A LARGE VERSION OF THE SPARROWHAWK. Two things to remember: Goshawk is *very* much bigger – nearer the size of a Buzzard – and it is a much rarer and more secretive bird. Many claims of Goshawk turn out to be large female Sparrowhawks. Goshawks breed deep in dense forests, where they are surprisingly elusive for such a large bird. Like Sparrowhawks, they have a fast, low flight when hunting, but will take much larger prey, including rabbits. Courtship display flights can be spectacular. The plumage is much the same as Sparrowhawk, but Goshawk has a slightly hooded appearance to the head, and more obvious white undertail coverts. Neither of these points is easy to see, and the size and bulk of the bird – including a more bulging hind wing – are the best features. But it's not easy! Juveniles, however, have vertical streaking on the underparts, whereas those of young Sparrowhawk are horizontal like the parents.

Basically looks and flies like a large Sparrowhawk. However, note the bulging rear edge of the wing (secondaries) – straighter on Sparrowhawk.

**Juvenile** (below left). Note underparts are vertically streaked (horizontal bars on Sparrowhawk).

**Adult** (above). Goshawks are shy, elusive birds that live in deep forest. Never forget that Goshawk is much rarer and that female Sparrowhawks can be pretty big!

THE BUZZARD IS BY FAR the commonest large bird of prey in Britain, though not often seen in the east of England, but is spreading even there. Equally at home in mountains, moors and farmland, sometimes perching on posts right by the roadside. It is equally often seen soaring way up in the sky in wild country, where it is often mistaken for an eagle. Eagles only occur in Scotland and the Western Isles (and one pair in the Lake District). So, a good rule: always assume a large bird of prey is a Buzzard until proved otherwise! Beware though that other species such as crows, gulls or even herons can soar up high in raptor-like fashion (see page 66). Beware also that Buzzard's plumage is extremely variable. Some of them can look almost white underneath, whilst others are very dark brown. There are all sorts of combinations in between. The paler forms usually have dark wing tips and "wrists" on the underwings. They have a mewing call.

Note: highly variable coloration. Birds of open country, Buzzards soar a great deal, often very high in the sky, with wings often held in a shallow V.

May be seen sitting on posts adjacent to a roadway. Buzzards feed mainly on small mammals, particularly rabbits, and will also take a large amount of carrion.

# OSPREY

A LARGE RAPTOR, AS BIG AS A BUZZARD, but slimmer and longer-winged; not as slender as a harrier. Both male and female are dark brown above, almost silky white below, with a few darker markings on the underwing, and a striking white forehead with dark "mask". This is a non variable plumage (makes a change for a large raptor!) and is very distinctive. Ospreys are dependent on water, since they feed on fish, which they catch in their talons. So, this is a pretty easy bird to identify. Not common, but the breeding population is healthy; restricted to Scotland (although measures are being taken to attract them to southern waters). Summer visitor, arriving in late March or April, and departing by September or early October. At either end of this migration period, Ospreys may drop in to fish at almost any inland lake or reservoir. The flight style is rather bow-winged, a little reminiscent of a large gull. Call: like so many raptors a rather feeble noise, in this case, a thin plaintive whistling.

The flight style is rather bow-winged, a little reminiscent of a large gull. Spectacular plunge dive, with feet held forward to catch fish, often submerging completely.

Male, female and juvenile all look much the same. Breeding almost entirely restricted to Scotland, but winters in Africa, so may turn up at inland waters farther south when migrating.

UNDOUBTEDLY THE COMMONEST AND MOST WIDESPREAD British bird of prey. The familiar motorway hawk, often seen hovering over the verges, and it breeds even in the middle of cities, where its prey is principally small birds such as house sparrows rather than the mice and voles that make up the bulk of its diet in the country. Males have bluish heads and rufous backs, while females are generally browner and more barred. Youngsters even more so. The call is a fast "keekeekeekeekee", often delivered from the air when the birds are indulging in their shallow-wingbeat, fast-flapping, display flights. Kestrels usually nest in holes and crevices – in trees, buildings or rocks (Sparrowhawks usually make a nest of twigs in a tree). Distinguished from Sparrowhawk by more pointed – falcon-shaped – wings, and habitual hovering when hunting, as well as very different plumage, if you get a good view. It is worth familiarizing yourself with the size and style of Kestrel, as this helps to identify the other less common British falcons.

Hovering flight over roadway verges or other areas of short grass. Kestrels will hover for prolonged periods, scanning the ground below before dropping onto prey.

Note long tail, long pointed wings. Fast-flapping, shallow display flight.

**Female** (above) is browner, barred with black. Same size as male.

**Male** (right) has bluish-grey head and grey tail with black tail band, and russet back.

# PEREGRINE

## 38–48 CM, 15–19 IN

THE LARGEST OF OUR FALCONS. Rather like a large stocky version of Hobby, but more barrel-chested and with shorter wings. Peregrines are incredibly fast in the dive or stoop when hunting, but not as acrobatic as Hobbies. Peregrines are also all-year-round birds, breeding on cliffs and rock faces, but sometimes descending to coastal marshes during the winter. Never seen in the same kind of wooded habitat as Hobbies. Numbers are steadily increasing and it may not be long before they begin to breed on city buildings as they do in parts of America. Male and female are bluish steely grey above, with horizontal bars on the underparts (Hobby's are vertical) and with very striking broad moustaches on a white cheek. The youngsters are browner and streakier. The call is the inevitable "kee kee kee", but with a Peregrine's accent! Funnily enough, one of the possible confusion species is feral pigeon, which can look surprisingly like a falcon (particularly Peregrine) when it is dashing away. Ironically, pigeons are among the Peregrine's favourite meals!

Barrel-chested and powerful. You wouldn't think you could mistake a feral pigeon for a Peregrine, but it happens!

**Adult** (below) – note strong black moustaches, horizontal barring on underparts. **Juvenile** (below left) is browner streaked than adult. Usually breeds on crags or cliffs.

As with many raptors, the female is larger than the male. It's called sexual dimorphism! It means she can take slightly larger prey and doesn't directly compete with the male.

# MERLIN
## 27–33 CM, 10.5–13 IN

MERLINS BREED ON WILD TREELESS MOORLANDS, and some of them descend to coastal marshes in the winter. Nowhere is this a common bird, and it tends to be elusive, often seen dashing away over the horizon. Your best chance of getting a decent view is of a bird resting on a post or rock at the coast between feeds, or if you happen to be close to a nest out on the moors (the nest is usually on the ground, among heather). The male is bluish-grey above, while female and young birds are brown. The most characteristic feature is its lack of moustaches, which all the other British falcons have to a varying degree. In fact, confusion is probably most likely with a young or female Sparrowhawk, which is also rather nondescript brown. Note the Merlin's more dashing flight style, and its preference for open habitat, where it feeds almost exclusively on small birds. You won't see a Merlin in a wood!

In flight, Merlins are fast and dashing, pursuing prey low over the ground then rising above them to strike. Compare streaked underparts with Sparrowhawk's horizontal bars.

**Female** (right), **male** (far right). Most distinctive feature when perched is absence of moustaches, but beware confusion with Sparrowhawk.

# HOBBY
### 30–36 CM, 12–14 IN

A SUMMER VISITOR ONLY. ARRIVES IN APRIL, gone by early October. Hobbies are about the same size as a Kestrel and – if you can't see plumage details – then Kestrel is the most likely confusion species. Hobby has long narrow wings, held in a slightly rakish scythe-like position: often likened to the silhouette of a large Swift. When hunting, it is very fast and acrobatic, sometimes suddenly changing direction as it zooms after large insects (dragonflies are a favourite and may be eaten while the bird is flying along) and sometimes small birds (particularly swallows or martins). Hobbies are fast! They rarely hover. They breed (not commonly) in woodlands, mainly in the southern half of England. Adult is deep bluish black above, with clear moustaches, broadly streaked underparts and rufous leggings. All very different from a Kestrel! Juveniles are a browner version, without the strong colours or markings, but with the same fast shape and style. Call: "keekeekeekee" (like so many small birds of prey!). See also Peregrine (page 63) which could be confused.

Breeding in heathland and southern woodlands, Hobbies nest in trees and can fly fast enough to catch swifts. Swallows and martins are among the birds most often taken.

Hobbies catch dragonflies in their claws, often holding them to the beak to be eaten in flight. Note rufous undertail.

**Juvenile** (above) lacks the **adult's** (above left) strong colours or markings, but has the same fast shape and style.

BIRDWATCHERS – EVEN EXPERIENCED ONES – sometimes make mistakes because they assume a distant bird (or flock of birds) is what they "expect" it to be. Assumptions can be dangerous! Not all large circling birds are raptors; not all V formation flocks are geese. A closer look through binoculars reveals the truth.

Soarers and circlers. These species are all capable of soaring way up in the sky in typical bird of prey fashion. It seems that even other birds are fooled, because they will often "mob" the raptor impersonator. Crows, in particular, seem to make mistakes! (Or maybe they just enjoy being belligerent.) Mind you, the frantic cawing of mobbing crows will often draw attention to a real raptor overhead.

Herring Gull

Great Black-backed Gull

Osprey

Grey Heron

Large gulls, Heron and Osprey: all may fly high and circle on thermals. Size at a distance is very difficult to judge, so you will have to attempt to make out the bird's shape and any markings.

Crows can themselves soar and circle and look like raptors, but when you see one (or more) mobbing a Buzzard, you realize they really haven't got true raptor style.

Buzzard

Use your ears. Birds often call in flight. Buzzards have a distinctive mewing call.

Carrion Crow

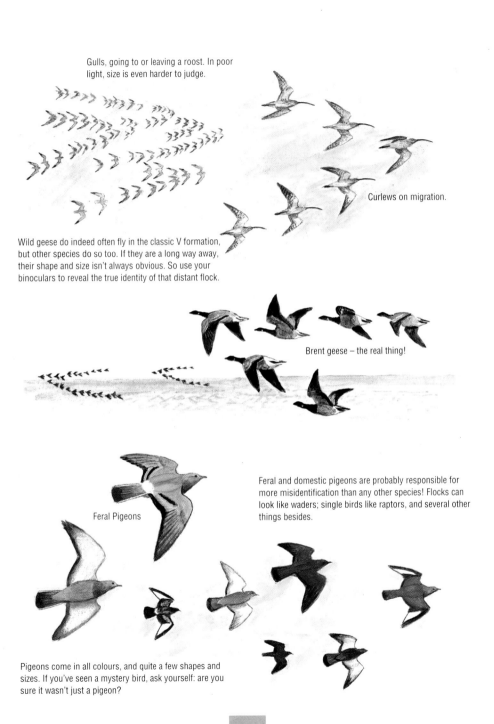

Gulls, going to or leaving a roost. In poor light, size is even harder to judge.

Curlews on migration.

Wild geese do indeed often fly in the classic V formation, but other species do so too. If they are a long way away, their shape and size isn't always obvious. So use your binoculars to reveal the true identity of that distant flock.

Brent geese – the real thing!

Feral Pigeons

Feral and domestic pigeons are probably responsible for more misidentification than any other species! Flocks can look like waders; single birds like raptors, and several other things besides.

Pigeons come in all colours, and quite a few shapes and sizes. If you've seen a mystery bird, ask yourself: are you sure it wasn't just a pigeon?

# RED GROUSE
## 38–41 CM, 15–16 IN

RED GROUSE ARE FOUND ONLY ON OPEN TREELESS MOORLAND in the north and western parts of Britain and Ireland. Like all game birds, they are basically a bit chicken-like and if you flush them they fly away with whirring wings, often giving an alarm call. They occur in similar regions to Black Grouse and Ptarmigan, but as with all game birds the type of habitat will often help you identify them. Black Grouse are generally near to wooded areas; Ptarmigan occur only on the mountain tops of Scotland. Ptarmigan always show white wings. Red Grouse male and female are overall deep reddish brown, with whitish underwings, which are quite conspicuous when they fly. The male is the redder of the two, and has a red comb above the eye. The alarm call is a cackling "kowk kok kok". Display call is often written as "go back back back". Grouse are larger than partridges (which rarely occur in the same kind of habitat anyway.)

The usual view – flying away! If they've got any sense they won't fly this high on a shooting day! Flushed, they fly away on whirring wings. Underwings are whitish.

**Male** (right) – darker reddish-brown than female, with larger red comb.

**Female** (below) - very like female Black Grouse, but remember Black Grouse prefer to be close to wooded areas; Red Grouse are birds of open moorland.

# BLACK GROUSE
MALE 53 CM, 21 IN; FEMALE 41 CM, 16 IN

SLIGHTLY BIGGER THAN RED GROUSE. Also lives on moor and heathland (but not in the south or east; also absent from Ireland) but generally prefers to be closer to woodland or forest than Red Grouse. Conifers and birch woods are favoured. In late winter and early spring they gather at "leks", where the Blackcocks display to Greyhens before mating. The males utter lovely cooing and bubbling calls. Males are very distinctive: black with lyre-shaped tails, and a gleaming white undertail shown off in the display. The hens are very similar to female Red Grouse, but are slightly larger, greyer, with a forked tail, and a faint wing bar on the upperwing. Black Grouse occur in similar habitat to Capercaillie in the Scottish pinewoods and are not dissimilar. Capercaillie male is huge. The female is smaller but still bigger than a female Black Grouse and also paler, gingery with more obvious barring (compare Capercaillie, page 71). Black Grouse sometimes visit grassy farmland to feed, particularly in winter.

**Blackcock** (left) – note double white wing bar. **Greyhen** (above) – note faint wing bar on upperwing. Greyer than female Red Grouse.

**Blackcock** gather at a lek early in the morning in early spring. One male will mate with several females.

**Blackcock** displaying to a **greyhen** at a lek. When they aren't displaying they can be very hard to see - often lurking in thick forest.

# PTARMIGAN

FOUND ONLY ON THE MOUNTAIN TOPS OF CENTRAL AND NORTHERN SCOTLAND. Most likely to be confused in summer with Red Grouse. Ptarmigan are slightly smaller, and always have white wings, which are usually visible even before the bird flies, if you can see it (they are beautifully camouflaged). In fact, if they are disturbed by people, they usually "freeze", relying on their camouflage rather than flying away. In breeding plumage, the male is darker than the female and has a red comb above the eye. In winter, the birds moult into almost completely white plumage, so that they blend into the snow. In autumn the males become greyer, and the white blotches begin to appear. Call is a short "croak" and it has a grating alarm call. Ptarmigans rarely come down from the mountain tops even in harsh winter weather. They feed on berries, seeds, plant shoots and leaves, and nest among heather and crowberry. The legs are feathered like those of Red Grouse.

Winter plumage **male** is almost completely white, with a red comb over the eye. In breeding plumage it is darker than the female, but it starts to turn grey in autumn.

The **female,** when incubating eggs, relies on her exquisite camouflage for protection.

# CAPERCAILLIE

MALE 86 CM, 34 IN; FEMALE 62 CM, 24 IN

FOUND ONLY IN PINE AND CONIFER FORESTS OF CENTRAL SCOTLAND. Despite being a very large bird it is very hard to see, unless you happen to find a lek, where, early on spring mornings, the males display and sometimes fight for the attention of females. The male is as big as a large turkey, and overall largely blackish. It could only really be confused with male Black Grouse, which can occur in the same forests and also sometimes perches in trees, as does the "Caper". Note that Caper really is much bigger and lacks the Black Grouse white undertail or wing bar (though Caper does have a small white shoulder patch). Female Capercaillie is much smaller than the male but still slightly bigger than a grouse. Compared with Black Grouse female, she is paler, with a sandy patch on the breast, more obvious delicate barring on the upper parts, and a rounded tail. Beware though that young Capercaillies – like all game bird chicks – can fly almost as soon as they are hatched.

The **male's** call is among the most absurd sounds in nature. It consists of a crescendo of bubbling noises – like champagne being poured from a bottle, and ending with a pop like the sound of champagne being uncorked.

**Female** is much smaller than male. If you see a small game bird that doesn't quite seem to fit the book. ask yourself: is it a flying, not fully-grown youngster? And look for its parents.

# RED-LEGGED PARTRIDGE

## 34 CM, 13.5 IN

THERE ARE TWO SPECIES OF PARTRIDGES IN BRITAIN: Red-legged and Grey. In flight, or seen scurrying through long vegetation, they can look very similar. But note that Red-legged Partridge is absent through most of western and northern Britain and does not occur in Ireland. It was originally introduced into Britain, and the further introduction of feral birds, plus the occurrence of the very similar Chukar Partridge, confuses the distribution, so it is best not to make assumptions. The two species favour similar farmland or open habitat – neither is likely on grouse moors – but they look very different when seen well. Note Red-legged's white face and black cheek edging (often the head is the only bit visible!) The black neck and red and black flank stripes are also quite different from Grey Partridge. The legs are indeed red (Grey's are yellowish) but that may be the last bit you look at! They are often seen in small groups and, when disturbed, they can run very fast as well as fly away. Call is "chuck chukar", repeated.

If disturbed, Red-legged Partridges are just as likely to run as fly. Alarm call is a sharp "kuk-kuk".

Bright white face, with black edging to cheeks, compared with sandy face of Grey Partridge, make it easy to distinguish from Grey, given a good view. Lacks dark belly patch of male Grey.

# QUAIL
18 CM, 7 IN

# GREY PARTRIDGE
30 CM, 12 IN

**QUAIL** IS A SUMMER VISITOR IN SMALL NUMBERS, though some years it is more numerous than others. Most likely in southern Britain. Call: a distinctive "quick kwi quick", sometimes written as "wet my lips" (though I can't really hear that myself!). If you hear this sound in late spring or summer coming from deep in a cornfield or impenetrable vegetation, it means a male Quail is in there somewhere. Your best chance of seeing it is simply to wait – it might just fly briefly. **Grey Partridge** found in similar habitat to Red-legged. Seems to be declining in many parts of the country, where you are more likely to see Red-leggeds and Chukars. Usually best spotted by scanning across fields of short grass or crops. Even then, they tend to crouch low when feeding, or sit still when disturbed. In flight, they are not easy to separate from Red-legged. Call is a grating "kerrr-ick". They are often particularly noisy at dusk.

**Quail (male** in foreground with **female** behind). Likeliest confusion is with young game birds. Flight is very fast, whirring and usually short. If you are lucky the bird might scuttle across open ground.

A decent view reveals that **Grey Partridge** has a sandy – not white and black face – and the underparts are indeed grey. Male has a black "horseshoe" belly patch.

**Grey Partridge (male,** left; **female,** above; much plainer **juvenile** behind). Favourite nesting site is under hedges or in thick fieldside verges.

# PHEASANT

FOUND IN WOODS, PARK AND FARMLAND IN MOST PARTS OF BRITAIN. Many of the pheasants in Britain are hardly wild birds at all, since they have been bred and released purely to be shot and eaten. Pheasants never were true natives, since they were first introduced from the far east back in Roman times. However, the plus side is that many Pheasant woodlands also support other wildlife. In any event, a cock pheasant is a very handsome bird and pretty unmistakable. Female is basically sandy brown with darker speckles, clearly larger than a partridge and with a long pointed tail. Pheasants do often interbreed with other more exotic races and species and it is therefore not unusual to see a bird that has non typical plumage. Some of them are almost black, others lack the usual head markings, or have added patches of colour. Flight always looks a bit clumsy, with whirring wingbeats and a glide that threatens to turn into a crash landing! The male has a short double crowing call: "kor-kok".

**Female.** Sandy brown, with long pointed tail, though not so magnificent as the male's. Nests on the ground in shelter of brambles, long grass.

**Male** is very variable – from almost black to pale. May not have white ring on neck. One male will try to gather a harem of several females.

# WATER RAIL
## 28 CM, 11 IN

BREEDS – VERY SECRETIVELY – IN MARSHY, REEDY AREAS, and additional birds fly in from the continent to winter in Britain. A bird that is probably more often heard than seen, and is probably far commoner than we realize. It is very secretive in its habits, creeping around silently, either deep in reedbeds or in shady undergrowth in damp areas, sometimes even along woodland streams. Its call is a rather panicky wheezing or squealing – sometimes likened to a piglet in pain! – or a sharp "pip". A sharp sudden noise such as a distant gun shot – or even a hand clap – will sometimes provoke a call and betray the bird's presence. If you do see one, you will appreciate its general resemblance to a juvenile Moorhen, but note its smaller size, the long thin red beak, greyer underparts and barred flanks. The young are more fawn coloured, and the beak is shorter, but they are very rarely seen (I've never seen one!).

**Juvenile.** More fawn coloured and with slightly shorter beak than adult, but very rarely seen.

**Adult.** The barred flanks are the part most likely to catch the eye as it skulks through cover. Seen from behind, it is a very thin bird, ideal for slipping between reeds!

WIDESPREAD ALL OVER BRITAIN IN JUST ABOUT ANY DAMP HABITAT, including park lakes and ditches. Absent only from high moorland, fast-flowing rivers and saltmarshes. Although Moorhens are so familiar, non birdwatchers seem to take time to sort them out from the almost equally common Coot. Adult Moorhens have a red and yellow beak, plus white areas on the flanks and the tail, and, although the rest of the body may look blackish, in fact it's a mix of dark blue and brown. Young Moorhens are the ones that can be a bit of a puzzle. They are simply brown and fawn, without any bright colours, and they are often skulky and merely seen scuttling into cover. This means they can be mistaken for Water Rails (page 75) or even some of the really rare crakes (the family to which Moorhen belongs). Really tiny Moorhen chicks are all black (rather perversely, Coot chicks have red heads). Adults swim and walk with a jerky head movement and flicking tail.
Call: a harsh "krrek" or "kittick".

**Juvenile** (right). It's a good rule that if you think you may have seen a rare crake or rail: ask yourself if are you sure it wasn't just a juvenile Moorhen?

**Adult.** Common on ponds and rivers, often feeds on land. Swims with jerky head-nodding; unlike coot, does not often dive, but capable of scooting underwater to avoid detection!

# COOT
### 38 CM, 15 IN

ALMOST AS COMMON AND WIDESPREAD AS MOORHEN, though there are parts of western Scotland where it is a scarce bird, and it generally prefers larger, more open water. Sometimes forms large flocks on lakes or reservoirs. Feeds largely on waterweeds, obtained by diving. Adults are black, with white beak and forehead shield (this is supposedly the "bald" part!). Small chicks are black but with bald red heads for the first few weeks. They soon attain juvenile plumage, which is – rather surprisingly perhaps – white on the underparts. At this time, they can resemble winter plumage small grebes (compare Slavonian and Black-necked Grebe, pages 12 and 14). The problem only occurs during a few autumn weeks, because Coot soon moult into adult all black plumage. The most common Coot call supposedly sounds like its name: an echoey "coot". It also gives a sharp "kik". Remember that Coot can fly, and that they sometimes go quite high and for a moment can look really puzzling, like some weird gangly duck, with trailing feet.

**Juvenile** has white underparts for a few weeks at the end of summer before moulting into adult plumage. Tiny chicks are downy and wispy, with bald red heads.

Coot often gather in flocks, especially in winter. They prefer deeper, more open water than moorhens, and dive to feed.

**Adult.** White shield above white beak. At a distance, the rounded shape of back is distinctive. Coot have feet with lobed webs on the toes. Moorhens have long, greenish-yellow toes.

# AVOCET

### 43 CM, 17 IN

THE SYMBOL OF THE RSPB, largely because it represents a great conservation success. Avocets returned to breed in East Anglia after the Second World War. Now, thanks to the provision of carefully managed and protected bird reserves, their numbers are increasing and spreading. However, the breeding population is still mainly in the south-eastern half of England, at well known sites. To breed and raise chicks successfully, they need very precise conditions that will enable their invertebrate food to survive. Wintering flocks – sometimes of several hundred – gather at favoured estuaries in Essex and some southern counties. Wandering birds may occur farther north or west, particularly during migration periods. A large, but supremely elegant wader, the Avocet's crisp black and white plumage and shape are completely distinctive and unmistakable! Younger birds have a browner caste to the back than the adults. The call is a ringing "kleep", rather more fluty than an Oystercatcher. The extraordinary upturned bill is used to search for shrimps by sweeping with swift sideways flicks through shallow water and thin mud.

Young birds are less "clean" on the back than the adults. Very young chicks are speckled grey and have tiny upturned bills. The nest is a shallow depression on mud.

Dazzlingly white in flight. Often calls – a ringing "kleep", rather more fluty than an Oystercatcher.

Adult (below). Avocets swim and upend like ducks as well as wade, and are found on estuaries, salt and brackish marshes. Feeding involves brisk sideways sweeps of the bill.

# OYSTERCATCHER

### 43 CM, 17 IN

OCCURS ALL YEAR ROUND. Found all round the coasts, on sandy beaches and mudflats. Breeds in a shallow scrape on the ground on shingly areas, including inland gravel pits, and has also moved inland to farmland, especially in some areas of Scotland, where it may be seen poking around on grassy meadows! In winter, huge numbers come to Britain, especially from Norway and Iceland. A large conspicuous wading bird which really can't be confused with anything else. Lapwing and Avocet are also black and white, but quite different in shape and pattern and certainly don't have the Oystercatcher's carrot-coloured bill and pink legs. In flight, it shows a strong white wing bar, which again makes it easy to identify even at a distance. In winter it has a thin white collar. The call is a loud piping "kleep kleep", often uttered in flight, or in a display in pairs, running together along the sand, bills pointed towards the ground. It feeds mostly on shellfish, especially cockles, which it hammers open with its powerful bill.

Easily recognized, the Oystercatcher is almost incapable of flying without calling noisily – a loud piping "kleep kleep".

In **winter** Oystercatchers develop a thin white collar. Thousands come to winter on Britain's estuaries and coasts from northern Europe.

Male and female are identical. The long, bright red bill and pink legs make it easy to distinguish from other black and white birds, notably Avocet and Lapwing.

# LITTLE RINGED PLOVER
## 15 CM, 6 IN

VERY SIMILAR TO RINGED PLOVER, and care should be taken when distinguishing the two. Ringed Plover is by far the commoner. Little Ringed Plover is only a summer visitor, arriving in March and usually gone by the end of September. Little Ringed also prefers inland nesting sites – especially gravel workings – and even on migration is almost never seen on the actual coast (though it may occur on suitable habitat near the sea). The differences from Ringed are as follows. It is indeed slightly smaller – especially the head. Adults have a golden eye ring (not easy to see until you get closer or use a telescope). Legs are duller straw colour, compared with adult Ringed's almost orange, and the bill is black compared with Ringed's orange with a black tip. Juveniles are similar to Ringed but retain the smaller head shape, have no white above the eye, and have duller legs. The absolute fail-safe is when the birds fly: Little Ringed has no white wing bar. Ringed does.

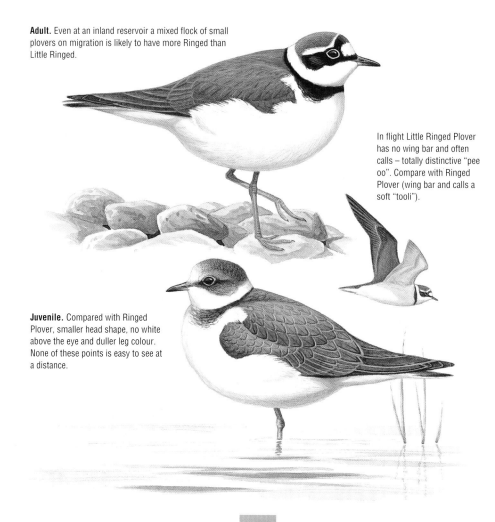

**Adult.** Even at an inland reservoir a mixed flock of small plovers on migration is likely to have more Ringed than Little Ringed.

In flight Little Ringed Plover has no wing bar and often calls – totally distinctive "pee oo". Compare with Ringed Plover (wing bar and calls a soft "tooli").

**Juvenile.** Compared with Ringed Plover, smaller head shape, no white above the eye and duller leg colour. None of these points is easy to see at a distance.

# RINGED PLOVER

## 19 CM, 7.5 IN

RINGED PLOVER IS THE COMMONEST OF THE SMALL BRITISH PLOVERS. It's a good idea to get to know Ringed Plover well, so that you can compare other species with it. It occurs all round the British coasts and also on inland waters with muddy or shingly shorelines, particularly during spring and autumn migration. They also breed, mainly on shingle beaches, but also sometimes on farmland near the coast, and rarely even inland. Call is a soft "tooli". The possible confusion species are Little Ringed Plover and the much rarer Kentish Plover. The first rule is to assume that any ringed type plover is a Ringed, until proved otherwise! In addition, Little Ringed does not occur on beaches and mudflats, and it is also only a summer visitor. Kentish Plover is a rare non breeding migrant, which occurs infrequently, mainly on south or east coast estuaries or beaches. It resembles juvenile Ringed Plover in having a broken breast band, but Kentish Plover has black legs. (For other differences see Kentish Plover, page 228.)

**Adult.** All plovers share the same basic shape: slightly dumpy bodied, relatively short-legged and short-billed, compared with other waders. Ringed can be used for comparison with others.

**Juvenile.** The breast band may even be "broken" like Kentish Plover, but note Ringed Plover's yellowish legs.

The simple distinction from Little Ringed Plover – note Ringed Plover has a wing bar.

# GOLDEN PLOVER

## 28 CM, 11 IN

THIS AND GREY PLOVER LOOK SIMILAR BUT HAVE VERY DIFFERENT HABITS. Golden Plovers breed on bleak moorlands, but winter in large flocks, usually on farmland or estuaries, often in company with Lapwings. In breeding plumage, they are yellowish-brown above – "golden" is a bit of an exaggeration – and black on the underparts. The northern race has more black than the southern. In winter, the black is replaced with whitish and the yellow upperparts become duller. Compare Grey Plover (opposite), which is not that dissimilar, though the upperparts are indeed grey, lacking yellow tones. Grey Plovers do not breed in Britain and occur only on coastal mudflats, and very rarely at inland waters on migration. Grey Plovers never occur in dense winter flocks like "Goldies". Identification problems would only really arise with single birds. In fact, Golden Plovers very rarely are on their own! Golden Plover is more slender than Grey Plover. In flight silvery white underwing is revealed – compare with Grey's black "armpit". Golden Plover's call is a fairly short "floo ee".

**Non breeding plumage.** In certain lights they might look rather less yellow than this individual and be confusable with Grey Plover. Usually in flocks in winter on estuaries and farmland.

**Juvenile.** Fast in flight. Note white underwing.

**Breeding plumage.** Northern race birds, most of which breed north of Britain, have black extending up onto throat and face. Breeds on upland moorland.

DOES NOT BREED IN BRITAIN, but birds may spend the summer on British estuaries. Does not visit dry habitat like Golden Plover; almost invariably seen on mudflats, beaches or estuaries, though occasional strays can turn up on inland waters. Summer plumage is most likely to be seen in late spring, as birds migrate north to their Arctic breeding grounds, or early in the autumn when they are returning south. At this time, quite large numbers sometimes occur, but they rarely flock together except at a high tide roost. Breeding and non breeding plumages are not dissimilar to Golden Plover, but at no time does Grey show yellow tinges, and in flight the black armpit is easy to see and diagnostic. Greys are also a little stockier and thicker necked than Golden. Call is a long almost mournful whistle "flee oo eee ", which carries a very long way, and often draws attention to birds flying overhead. Juveniles have neater white spots on the upperparts.

**Adult in breeding plumage**. Americans call them Black-bellied Plover. Presumably they were named in summer! Some birds spend the summer in Britain, but do not breed.

**Juvenile**. Note Grey Plover's black "armpit" (axillaries) – very easy to see when it flies. Compare with Golden Plover.

**Non breeding plumage**, when it really is grey. Juveniles have neater white spots on the upperparts. Not likely to be seen in flocks except at high tide roosts,

# DOTTEREL

A VERY ATTRACTIVE PLOVER WITH DISTINCTIVE HABITS. A summer visitor only. There are really only two circumstances in which you are likely to see Dotterels: on the tops of mountains in the Highlands of Scotland, where they breed, or, if you are lucky enough to come across or hear of a small flock – called a "trip" – on spring migration. There are certain sites in England where birds seem to stop off nearly every year, sometimes staying for a few days to feed in spring wheat fields. Odd birds may also occur on autumn migration – usually on stubble fields at coastal sites – but they are pretty rare. Dotterel is a medium-sized plover – bigger than Ringed but smaller than Lapwing – and superficially a little like winter plumage Golden Plover. However, if at all well seen, they are distinctive: no other wader has the vivid white eyebrow – which is sometimes all you can see above the vegetation – or the white breast band and orange belly. Another wader that doesn't wade.

**Juvenile** – a sort of washed-out version of the adult, with all markings much fainter.

Note no wing bar in flight – most other plovers have one. Dotterel is a rare summer visitor, breeding on mountain tops in the Scottish highlands.

**Adult.** The females are actually brighter than the males. Males do most of the incubating and caring for the young and therefore need to be less conspicuous on the nest.

# LAPWING

### 30 CM, 12 IN

THE COMMONEST AND THEREFORE THE MOST FAMILIAR of the larger British plovers . It is sometimes known as Green Plover – because of its plumage – or Peewit – after its call. It is a widespread – but possibly decreasing – breeding bird on farmland, low moorland and the edges of large lakes. In winter, large flocks are a common sight on estuaries and coastal marshes and – during cold spells and snow – they often undertake "weather movements", when they may be seen flying high, even over the middle of cities, probably on their way to milder conditions in the west country, Ireland or even Spain. On the breeding grounds, the males have a wonderful tumbling display flight, during which the wings make a humming noise which gives the bird its name. It's *not* "flap wing", though to be honest that too would be appropriate, as the flight is indeed flappy! The winter flocks may be mixed with Golden Plovers, so it's always worth scanning through them.

The black and white plumage and round-winged twinkly flight style makes a flock of Lapwings identifiable even at long distances.

Round wings and floppy wingbeats. Males in spring can be seen in tumbling display flight over fields.

**Adult in breeding plumage**. At close range equally unmistakable. No other wader has the outrageous crest and glossy green plumage, though juveniles have a scalier look and shorter head plumes.

DOESN'T BREED IN BRITAIN, BUT WINTERS IN LARGE NUMBERS: flocks sometimes number several thousands. They begin to arrive in autumn, and leave in spring, and may show tinges of breeding plumage, with a variable amount of red on the underparts. Confusion could occur with single birds or small groups looking a bit like Curlew Sandpipers or even Grey Phalarope. The latter is easily dismissed, since – as far as I know – Grey Phalarope has never occurred in Britain in breeding plumage! Knot is clearly larger, shorter legged, and straighter billed than Curlew Sandpiper. Winter or juvenile plumage Knot are basically grey above and white below. This is similar to other small waders, such as Dunlin, but again note that Knot is bigger, stockier and straighter billed. In flight, it also shows a pale rump, which Dunlin lack. Call is a rather subdued "knut", rarely given or heard. A cloud of Knot, veering over mudflats or coming into a roost is among the great wader spectacles of the world.

**Adult breeding plumage.** Any large flock, apart from in winter, may have birds showing variable amounts of red.

**Juvenile** – like non breeding plumage but neater upperparts feathers – seen only in autumn.

**Non breeding plumage.** A typical grey and white wader, but slightly bigger and stockier than Dunlin and with a straighter bill. In flight it shows a pale rump.

# SANDERLING

### 20 CM, 8 IN

Doesn't breed in Britain but is nevertheless a common sight on sandy beaches, as it – usually in a small busy flock – chases the edge of the sea, as if playing tag with the waves. This behaviour is typical of Sanderling, and makes them easy to identify. However, occasionally, stray birds do occur away from beaches, even on inland reservoirs, and there they can be more of a puzzle. In late spring and early autumn, birds may be in total or partial breeding plumage, with scaly rufous upperparts and upper breast, and white below: not that different from some Dunlin or Little Stint. Sanderling is considerably larger than a stint, and even a little bigger than a Dunlin. It is rather plump and short legged, with a rather short straight bill. The call is a short "pip pip", not unlike a Little Stint, but quite different from a Dunlin. In practice, identification problems rarely arise, because Sanderling are far more likely to be seen on the beach chasing waves, than mixing with other waders.

**Adult non breeding**. The winter plumage becomes increasingly whiter, till they look positively ghostly, with just a black shoulder mark. Feeds on shorelines, usually chasing the waves in small flocks.

**Juvenile** – similar to non breeding but more spangled, neater upperparts feathers. Seen in autumn.

**Adult in full breeding plumage** – partial plumages also occur from late spring to early autumn. An active, busy little bird, always running to and fro at the wave's edge.

# LITTLE STINT

## 13 CM, 5.25 IN

ANOTHER SMALL WADER THAT IS ONLY A MIGRANT IN BRITAIN. Scarce in spring but more frequent in autumn. Often with Curlew Sandpipers and Dunlin, and thus allowing direct comparison. Little Stint is clearly quite a bit smaller than Dunlin, with a shorter straighter beak. It has a very busy feeding action, constantly picking at the mud. In breeding plumage, the upperparts have a foxy tinge to them, and this can extend onto the breast. In this plumage, confusion could arise with breeding plumage Sanderling, which just might occur at the same locations (compare Sanderling). But Sanderling are clearly larger, and generally prefer the seashore. Little Stints definitely prefer shallow muddy wetlands or sheltered estuaries. Juvenile Little Stints, when seen closely and in good light, show an ochre tinge to the upperparts, and a pair of white "braces" down the back. Young Dunlin also have this feature, but rarely so cleanly, and again I stress that Little Stint really are little. The call is a rather feeble, short "pip".

**Juvenile** – a pair of white "braces" on the mantle are key feature – one of them just visible here. Most birds seen in autumn will be in this plumage.

**Full winter plumage** isn't often seen in Britain. Smooth grey and white – just like many other small waders, but Little Stint really is little!

**Breeding plumage** – most likely to be seen in late summer/early autumn when birds are returning from the Arctic. Feeds on shallow muddy wetlands and estuaries.

# TEMMINCK'S STINT

14 CM, 5.5 IN

TEMMINCK'S STINT IS A MUCH RARER BIRD THAN LITTLE STINT. A very few pairs breed in the wilds of Scotland where it nests usually in sedge or marsh grasses. A few migrants pass through Britain each year, particularly in May, and again a few in August or September. Temminck's Stint prefers marshy fresh water habitat, and sometimes turns up on quite tiny wetlands inland, as well as near the coast. In spring, the upperparts are a similar colour to Little Stint though a little less reddish, and with rounder feathers, giving a slightly smoother look. Autumn birds are much smoother, with a smudgy breast band that makes it look a little like tiny Common Sandpipers (see page 105), though it isn't confusable with that species. The simple way to separate Temminck's from Little is to look at the leg colour. Temminck's has relatively pale yellowy legs. Little Stint's are black. Temminck's has a soft trilling call (unlike Little Stint's "pip") and a characteristic towering flight. It is also generally a less busy feeder than Little.

**Juvenile** (right). Only seen in autumn. Compared with Little Stint in all plumages, Temminck's is smoother and has yellowy legs.

**Adult non breeding plumage** (left). The smudgy breast band makes it look a bit like a tiny Common Sandpiper. Frequents fresh water margins on migration.

**Adult breeding plumage.** The later in spring it is, the more "spangly" the feathers will be. Breeds mostly in northern Europe, with a very few pairs nesting in Scotland.

# CURLEW SANDPIPER

19 CM, 7.5 IN

THE SPECIES THAT IS PROBABLY MOST CONFUSED WITH DUNLIN, since they are about the same size and share some other characteristics. First rule: Curlew Sandpipers are only migrants, which pass through Britain in spring and autumn, so don't expect them in winter! In May, or late July or early August, they are likely to show at least some signs of breeding plumage, notably rich red patches on their underparts, different from Dunlin. Only other wader to show that colour is breeding plumage Knot. Knot is larger, shorter legged, and straight billed (see page 86). Juvenile Curlew Sandpipers pass through in late August and September. They are grey above and white below, therefore similar to juvenile or wintry Dunlin. Note the Curlew Sand's slightly longer legs, smoothly decurved bill and softer grey back colour, with rounder feather shapes than a Dunlin, and gentle peachy wash on the breast. All these are subtle points. One feature is diagnostic: when the bird flies it shows a square white rump. The call is a soft "churrup".

A party could include an **adult in winter** (right), adult in partial breeding plumage (far right), with varying degrees of red on underparts and a few more in between!

**Juvenile** (left). Compare with Dunlin. It would be easier if it flew! Curlew Sands have a white rump, and often share habitat with Dunlin, allowing direct comparison.

**Adult in full breeding plumage** – alas the least likely plumage to be seen in Britain, for Curlew Sand is a passage migrant only.

# DUNLIN
## 17–19 CM, 6.5–7.5 IN

THE MOST WIDESPREAD SMALL BRITISH WADER. Knowing Dunlin is really the key to identifying the others. Small numbers breed on high moorlands, but you are far more likely to know them from coastal locations, or inland reservoirs or sewage farms – both on migration and during the winter when large flocks occur. All plumages occur at these places. Breeding plumage is distinctive enough, with rufous upperparts and black belly. Juveniles lack the black. Winter plumage becomes basically grey above and white below, in common with many waders! Familiarize yourself with the size, shape and bill and leg length of Dunlin – the overall jizz. Note that Dunlin has a fairly long bill, which is slightly kinked downwards at the tip. The call is a buzzy "dzeee", which is hard to write down, but once heard is not difficult to recognize. As with all waders, call is very helpful to identification. The call will often clinch the species, so try to get to hear them and know them.

**Juvenile.** No black on belly, but the feathers look very neat and "clean". The species breeds on upland moorland.

The plumage becomes greyer and smoother as winter progresses until they become the quintessential "little dull grey and white wader". Getting to know Dunlin jizz is the key to identification.

**Adult in breeding plumage.** Rufous on the back and with striking black belly patch – but birds occur in all plumage stages and often look less smart than this one!

# PURPLE SANDPIPER

## 21 CM, 8.25 IN

A WINTER VISITOR, WITH RATHER ODD HABITS, which fortunately help to identify it. Purple Sands only ever occur on rocky shorelines, or occasionally on jetties by the sea . They are absent in summer: they breed in the Arctic. Their plumage is hardly purple, more a sort of dark bluey grey. It is smoothest in mid-winter, becoming scalier as breeding dress appears. At all times, they have yellow legs, which separates them from any possible confusion species. They are most similar to Dunlin, but are a little larger and clearly dumpier, though they too have a slightly decurved beak, which is yellow at the base. They are typically rather relaxed birds, often sleeping, which makes them very hard to spot among rocks and seaweed. They have a soft chirruping call, which can hardly be heard above the noise of the waves. Very rarely, a Purple Sandpiper may stray to an inland reservoir, but if it does, it is almost certain to be on a rocky – or even concrete – shoreline.

**Juvenile.** Often asleep by day, Purple Sandpipers can be difficult to see among outcrops of rock and seaweed. Most active immediately after rocks have been uncovered by tide.

**Winter plumage.** Purple Sandpipers have a smooth appearance. Often occur in small parties, sometimes feeding with Turnstones. Swims readily.

**Breeding plumage** is dark, more scaly in appearance, but there is little sign of purple! Yellow legs and slightly decurved beak with yellow base. Larger and dumpier than Dunlin.

A GOOD APPROACH IF YOU SEE A WADER YOU CAN'T IMMEDIATELY IDENTIFY is to eliminate the ones you know it isn't! Make a note of habitat – some waders prefer seashore, some open mudflats and others fresh water marshes. Also listen for calls.

Knot

Purple Sandpiper

Little Stint

Ruff

Sanderling

Dunlin

Temminck's Stint

Curlew Sandpiper

Turnstone

In winter in particular many birds lose their distinctive plumage features and become basically grey – or brown – and white, so try to become aware of the differences in their shapes and sizes.

Black-tailed Godwits

Curlew

Redshanks

Greenshanks

Dunlin

Bar-tailed Godwits

Dunlin

Grey Plover

Redshank

Knot

Sanderling

Little Stints

Dunlin

Ruff

Golden Plovers

# RUFF

MALE RUFF IN BREEDING PLUMAGE is one of the most striking birds. However, non breeding birds can be a real identification problem, especially as the females (Reeves) are much smaller than males and look as if they ought to be a completely different species. If you are really puzzled by a small to medium-sized wader, ask yourself is it a Ruff or Reeve? First, notice the shape: slightly pot-bellied with a rather slender neck and small head, with shortish slightly downcurved bill. Then, note markings – or rather – the lack of them on the wings and rump. Wing bar is very faint. The rump is dark, but beneath is a sort of horseshoe-shaped white upper tail band. Sometimes, this appears split, and sometimes it seems to join. There are several other waders that can look a bit like Ruffs or Reeves – from Dunlin to Redshank to Wood Sandpipers – but none of them show this combination of very faint wing bar and horseshoe tail band.

The plumage of **non breeding** Ruff is generally a rather soft apricot buff, smooth on the underparts and extending right down to the lower belly (most other small waders have white underparts) and scaly on the back.

The leg colour is rather variable: sometimes quite strikingly yellow or orange (which often causes confusion with Redshank), while others are dull brown. Most numerous on spring and autumn passage.

Each spring a small number of **males** are seen in breeding plumage, but more often they have partial ruffs. Ruff prefer shallow pools; even quite dry areas, such as ploughed fields.

# WOODCOCK
34 CM, 13.5 IN

WOODCOCK – AS THE NAME IMPLIES – PREFER HABITATS WITH TREES. Your best chance of seeing them is at dawn or dusk, in spring and early summer, when the males make their regular display flights known as "roding". To be honest, you will be very lucky to see Woodcock on the ground, as they like dark places and their camouflage is superb. They may look momentarily like an owl. If you are lucky enough to get a close view, notice the cross barring on the dark crown, quite unlike a Snipe's stripes. There is a certain amount of migrational movement round Britain, and birds also arrive from the continent in autumn. At such times – particularly in October on the east coast – Woodcock may be flushed from more open habitat, such as sand dunes or meadows by the sea, the same sort of places you may also see Snipe. They will not utter the Snipe's distinctive harsh call, being either silent or maybe giving a soft grunt.

Breeds in some forested areas, particularly heathland with nearby conifers. Most likely to be seen at dusk or dawn, spring or early summer, in "roding" display flight.

Surprisingly slow wingbeats – a bit owl-like – and makes soft clicking noises. Compared with Snipe, Woodcock is larger, has rounder wings and slower, straighter flight.

Larger and more barrel-chested than Snipe, but with very similar plumage. Note cross-barred head. If disturbed, they dash away through the trees and soon disappear.

# COMMON SNIPE

## 27 CM, 10.5 IN

SNIPE HAVE A VERY DISTINCTIVE LOOK AND SHAPE. Very long straight bill, very short legs, and dark heavily streaked plumage. Only Woodcock shares this look (see page 95). Generally, Snipe are rather secretive, feeding at the edges of marshy pools or in boggy ground. They breed in damp meadows, marshes and on moorland all over Britain; larger numbers winter on lowland wet areas. They avoid the seashore. You are most likely to see them feeding out in the open on muddy pool edges in autumn. Otherwise, you more usually see Snipe dashing away from you after being flushed. Call: a harsh "scraarp", almost impossible to write down but once heard easily recognized. On the breeding grounds, they have a wonderful towering display flight, producing a strange throbbing humming sound (drumming ) by vibrating their outer tail feathers. They also have a high- pitched "chip chip" call. Woodcock are larger and prefer dryer habitat. Jack Snipe are smaller, winter visitors , much rarer and even more secretive (see Jack Snipe opposite).

Snipe fly with a very fast zigzag style and almost invariably call: a harsh "scraarp", difficult to describe, but once heard, easily recognized.

Snipe feed at the edges of marshy pools or in boggy ground, using their long bills to probe for worms.

To be honest, you don't often see Snipe posing like this – you're more likely to see them dashing away from you after being flushed.

# JACK SNIPE
## 19 CM, 7.5 IN

COMMON SNIPE'S RARE LITTLE COUSIN! Jack Snipe are winter visitors to Britain. They appear in September and October and have usually left by April. They like the same kind of damp habitat as Snipe but you are lucky to see one unless you literally almost tread on it. If you are lucky enough to see one in the open, it will usually be feeding along the edge of a marsh or sitting quietly almost hidden in the reeds. Seen well – compared with Common Snipe – note the more obvious double stripes on the head and along the back, shorter bill, the even squatter shape, and feet that look a size too big for its body! Certain marshes seem to be favourite wintering places for Jack Snipe and may have a small population all winter – but in nothing like the numbers that Common Snipe occur. The only place you are likely to record more than one or two in a day are the northern isles (Shetland or Orkney) in October when migrants are arriving.

The escape flight is straight – not zigzagging like Snipe) and usually low and short, before it drops back into cover and defies you to flush it again.

The feature most likely to attract your attention is its habit of bobbing on the spot, as if it were on a small spring. Jack Snipe are silent.

# BLACK-TAILED GODWIT

## 41 CM, 16 IN

THERE ARE TWO BRITISH SPECIES OF GODWIT: Black-tailed and Bar-tailed. They are both large waders, near to the size of a Whimbrel, not quite so big as a Curlew. They share similar basic plumage: brown above, and brick red below in breeding dress; brown above, whitish below in non breeding. They may occur together, in similar habitats, mainly muddy estuaries, and occasionally fresh water. By far the simplest way to tell them apart is to wait till they fly or preen, when they reveal their wing and tail markings. Black-tailed Godwit has a vivid broad white wing bar, a white rump and a broad black tail band. Bartail has a plain brown upperwing, and a less vivid white rump (V shaped ) and – as the name implies – a barred tail (see Bar-tailed, opposite).

Each year, a few pairs of Black-tailed Godwits breed in Britain in damp pastures, usually in east coast counties. Their display flights are very conspicuous, with much loud calling and singing: "reeka reeka, kweeit, weddy witoo" etc !

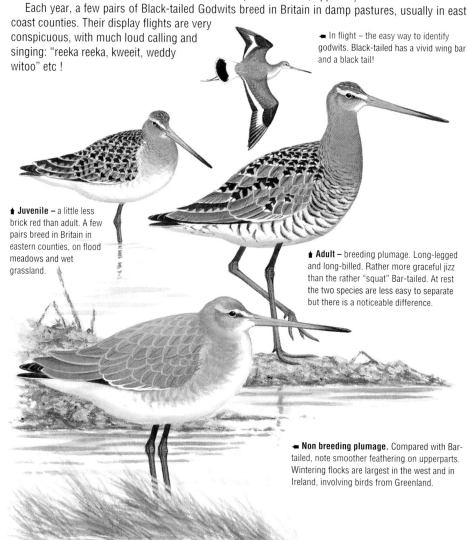

← In flight – the easy way to identify godwits. Black-tailed has a vivid wing bar and a black tail!

⬆ **Juvenile** – a little less brick red than adult. A few pairs breed in Britain in eastern counties, on flood meadows and wet grassland.

⬆ **Adult** – breeding plumage. Long-legged and long-billed. Rather more graceful jizz than the rather "squat" Bar-tailed. At rest the two species are less easy to separate but there is a noticeable difference.

← **Non breeding plumage.** Compared with Bar-tailed, note smoother feathering on upperparts. Wintering flocks are largest in the west and in Ireland, involving birds from Greenland.

BASICALLY SIMILAR IN LOOKS AND HABITS TO BLACK-TAILED. Does not breed, but large numbers winter in Britain. The plumages are similar to Black-tailed, but they are easily told apart when the wing and tail patterns can be seen – Bar-tailed has a plain upperwing and barred tail. In flight, the Bar-tailed's pattern is more similar to a Curlew or Whimbrel, but both have down-curved beaks and quite different calls. In flocks, especially on migration, Bartails often give a slightly yapping "kirrick" calls. If birds are feeding and hiding their characteristic wing and tail markings, they can still be separated from Black-tailed Godwit by their different shape: Bar-tailed is rather squat looking, with shorter legs and a slightly upturned bill. Also, note the back feathers are rather coarse and more pointed (like a Curlew's), compared with the softer smoother look of Black-tailed. Although Bartails generally favour estuaries and sea shores, flocks on spring migration are often seen arriving over the south coast and carrying on inland. Occasionally they are spotted heading north even over cities.

◀ Note plain upperwing – pale rump extends up back (square and brighter in Black-tailed) and tail is indeed barred, but rather dull.

⬇ **Juvenile** – very similar to non breeding plumage.

⬆ **Non breeding plumage.**
Compared with Black-tailed, note "squatter" jizz, upturned bill, shorter legs and coarser back feathering.

➡ **Breeding plumage.** In spring and early autumn, birds may be in breeding plumage, but it is more frequently seen in its brown above, white below non breeding dress.

# WHIMBREL
## 41 CM, 16 IN

A SUMMER VISITOR TO BRITAIN; small numbers breed on moorland in Scotland and the northern isles (especially Shetland). On passage, in spring and autumn, it is quite a frequent visitor to estuaries and coastal marshes, and occasionally inland. A few stay all summer, and odd ones very occasionally winter. The plumage is very similar to Curlew, but note smaller size, shorter less decurved bill, and the pale stripe on a dark crown. Unfortunately, none of these features may be immediately obvious if the bird is flying. Listen for the call, a staccato high-pitched whistle, given as many as seven times in rapid succession – "whi whi whi" etc. One of their local names is the Seven Whistler (but it doesn't have to be seven!) This is quite different from Curlew's call. (However – just to confuse matters – Whimbrel do occasionally utter a "curlew" call as well). Flight pattern is similar to Bar-tailed Godwit and – since the species are about the same size – try to see the decurved bill on flying birds.

Note shorter bill, smaller size than Curlew, and has a quite different call. Similar flight pattern to Bar-tailed Godwit, so try to see the bill!

Note the crown stripes, which distinguish it from Curlew. If only they were always so easy to see! Mostly a passage migrant to coasts and estuaries.

# CURLEW

53–58 CM, 21–23 IN

THE LARGEST BRITISH WADER. Large size, long down-curved bill, and unchanging plumage – always streaky brown above and white below – make this a familiar and easily identified bird. It even calls its own name! Breeds on moorlands and damp pastures in many parts of Britain, where it nests on the ground in a hollow among the grass. Larger numbers winter on estuaries, saltmarshes and farmland. Rather uncommon on inland waters on passage. On the breeding grounds, also has a wonderful bubbling song, delivered during the display flight, which is curiously fluttery and dainty for such a big bird. The most obvious confusion species is its small cousin the Whimbrel (see Whimbrel, opposite), which is a summer visitor only (very rare indeed in winter), smaller, shorter billed and with stripes on a dark crown. The calls are quite different, and fortunately both species almost invariably do call a lot. A flock of Curlews on migration often fly in V formation and could be mistaken for distant geese or large gulls (see pages 120–121)

Not easy to differentiate from Whimbrel in flight – note the larger size, more decurved bill and hope that it will call!

Britain's largest wader, Curlews have the same plumage in both summer and winter. Bill lengths vary and some look considerably larger even than this bird shows.

# REDSHANK

28 CM, 11 IN

ARGUABLY THE COMMONEST AND MOST WIDESPREAD OF BRITISH WADERS, breeding in damp places, both near the coasts and – in smaller numbers – inland. It is a medium-sized wader, larger than a Dunlin but much smaller than a Curlew. A species that you should really get to know well, so that you can compare others with it. Two things always identify Redshank. One is the bright white trailing edge to the upperwing (no other common wader has this) with white rump extending up the back, and the second is their distinctive call – a ringing "tew wu wu". There are several other waders that can be mistaken for Redshank – or vice versa – but there are clear differences when seen well. Non breeding Ruff (or Reeve): no wing markings, white oval on upper tail. Greenshank: greenish legs, paler greyer plumage. Wood Sandpiper: plain wings and square white rump. This latter confusion often arises with young Redshank, whose legs are less bright, more yellowy, and they have spottier upperparts. (For more see those species).
Breeds widely and larger numbers winter.

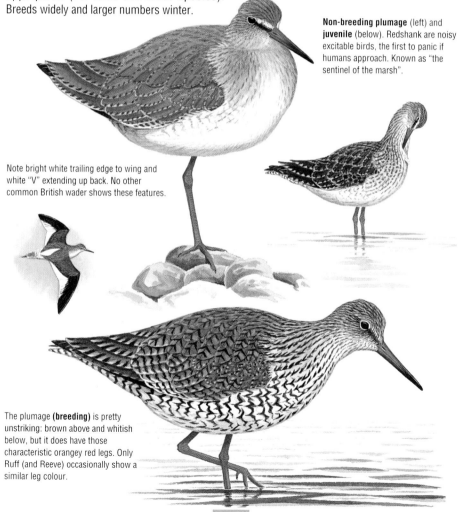

Non-breeding plumage (left) and juvenile (below). Redshank are noisy excitable birds, the first to panic if humans approach. Known as "the sentinel of the marsh".

Note bright white trailing edge to wing and white "V" extending up back. No other common British wader shows these features.

The plumage (breeding) is pretty unstriking: brown above and whitish below, but it does have those characteristic orangey red legs. Only Ruff (and Reeve) occasionally show a similar leg colour.

# SPOTTED REDSHANK

### 30 CM, 12 IN

DOES NOT BREED IN BRITAIN. A passage migrant, but not in very large numbers, mainly in southern areas, where large gatherings may occur in early autumn on estuaries, coastal marshes and occasionally on inland waters. Basically similar size to Redshank, and with red legs, but has quite a range of plumages. Breeding plumage is almost black with just a few small white spots. Non breeding adult plumage is soft pale grey above and white below. Juveniles are brown above and are most similar to common Redshank. The easiest ways to tell them apart are as follows: Spotted Redshank has a plain upperwing (no wing bar); the bill is slightly longer and thinner; it has a narrow pale stripe above the eye and the legs are darker red. The call is quite different. Spotted Redshank give a clear "tchuit". The only other confusion species is Greenshank, which also lacks any wing markings. Note Greenshank's green legs, different shape and distinctive call (see Greenshank, page 104).

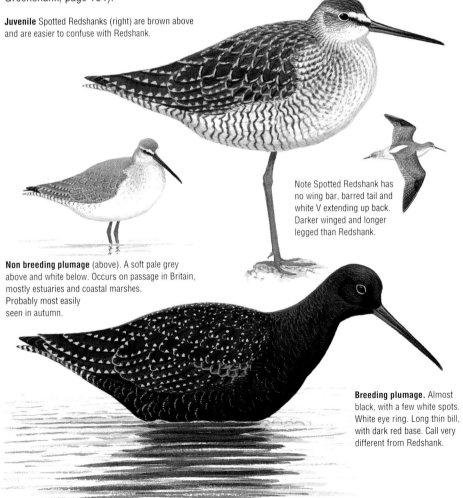

**Juvenile** Spotted Redshanks (right) are brown above and are easier to confuse with Redshank.

Note Spotted Redshank has no wing bar, barred tail and white V extending up back. Darker winged and longer legged than Redshank.

**Non breeding plumage** (above). A soft pale grey above and white below. Occurs on passage in Britain, mostly estuaries and coastal marshes. Probably most easily seen in autumn.

**Breeding plumage.** Almost black, with a few white spots. White eye ring. Long thin bill, with dark red base. Call very different from Redshank.

A FEW BREED IN MOORLAND AND BOGS OF SCOTLAND, but best known as a passage migrant in good numbers to coastal marshes and inland waters, with muddy or shingly shorelines. However, rarely do very many occur together in the same place. Slightly bigger than Redshank and with a squatter, less slender, look. The legs are indeed a rather greyish-green and the bill is also greyer than Redshank, a little thicker and slightly upturned. The plumage is greyer above and whiter below. This pale look helps pick out Greenshank even at a distance. Twisting and erratic rapid flight. In flight, there is no white wing bar or trailing edge, but there is a white rump extending up the back. This is a similar flight pattern to Spotted Redshank, so note leg colour and listen for the call. Greenshank gives a clear "tu tu tu", with a drier less ringing quality than Redshank. Often chases insects across the surface of shallow water, looking rather as if it is hoovering!

**Adult non-breeding** (above). **Juvenile** (far left) on back has slightly more regular pattern of dark feathers. In flight, note white rump extending up back and compare with Redshank and Spotted Redshank.

**Breeding plumage.** A paler bird than Redshank, slightly bigger, with thicker upturned bill. Outside the breeding season, a bird of estuaries, saltmarshes and the edges of inland waters.

# COMMON SANDPIPER
## 20 CM, 7.75 IN

A SMALL WADER WHICH IS A SUMMER VISITOR TO BRITAIN, breeding near streams, rivers and lakes, in moorland and hill country. It also occurs as a passage migrant at inland waters, including concrete sided reservoirs, and at coastal marshes. However, it very rarely feeds out on mudflats, more typically sticking to creek edges or banks, even when they are dry and stony. Rather nondescript plumage: soft olive-brown above and white below, with smudged sides to the breast. However, it does have a very distinctive style, bobbing and wagging its tail as it walks, and even at rest (known as teetering). In flight, it holds its wings down, and flits over the water with a flick and glide movement. It almost invariably calls as it flies: a thin "sweeweeweewee". All in all, one of those birds whose jizz and habits are more distinctive than its plumage. On the ground, it is not dissimilar to both Green and Wood Sandpipers, but both those species show plain upperwings and conspicuous square white rumps in flight.

In flight, the wings are held down as it flits over the water with a flick and glide movement. No white rump. Calls as it flies.

**Juvenile.** In summer it occurs on upland streams: as a migrant it turns up on inland waters such as reservoirs, as well as coastal marshes, where it feeds in creeks.

**Breeding plumage.** Olive-brown above, white below. Note smudged breast. Distinctive jizz, constantly bobbing and wagging tail as it walks along the edge of streams and other areas of water.

## 23 CM, 9 IN

BASICALLY, A DARK VERSION OF THE COMMON SANDPIPER. The upperparts are really nearer black than green (in fact, they are very dark olive tinged). Has very occasionally bred in northern Britain, but is mainly a passage migrant, especially in early autumn, and a few winter in the south. Easily separated from Common Sandpiper when it flies by black wings (above and below) and gleaming white rump. It also invariably gives a rather panicky "tweet wheet weet" call. Green Sandpipers occur on inland waters and tidal creeks and have a tendency to hide away under banks, or seemingly always round the next bend! If seen with Common Sandpiper it is obvious that Green is a little larger and bulkier, but this isn't always obvious with a single bird. Wood Sandpiper is about the same size, but prefers shallow fresh marshes, has less black upperparts and a quite different call (see Wood Sandpiper).

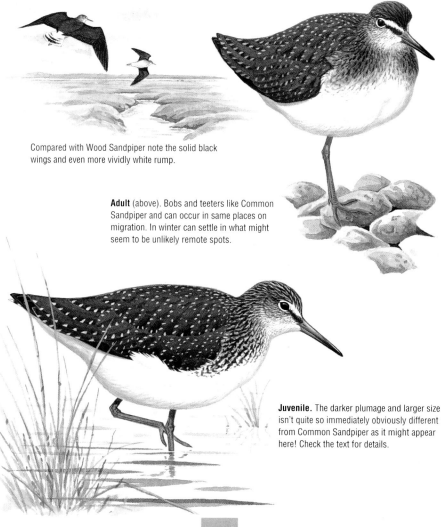

Compared with Wood Sandpiper note the solid black wings and even more vividly white rump.

**Adult** (above). Bobs and teeters like Common Sandpiper and can occur in same places on migration. In winter can settle in what might seem to be unlikely remote spots.

**Juvenile.** The darker plumage and larger size isn't quite so immediately obviously different from Common Sandpiper as it might appear here! Check the text for details.

# WOOD SANDPIPER

## 20 CM, 8 IN

A FEW PAIRS BREED IN REMOTE BOGGY AREAS OF SCOTLAND AND THE NORTHERN ISLES, but it is best known as a passage migrant, more common in autumn than spring. Prefers fresh water marshes, where it will more readily wade in shallow water than Common or Green Sandpipers. Size and plumage similar to Green Sandpiper, but the upperparts of Wood are browner, with more distinct spotting and clearer feather edges, and paler legs, which can look quite yellowish. Towering flight if flushed. In flight, it too has a square white rump, but the wings are brown above, and much paler underneath than Green Sandpiper. The call is a very distinctive: a dry "chiff if if". Juvenile looks very like adult. Juvenile Redshank look not dissimilar to Wood Sandpiper – they are shorter billed and spottier on the back than adult Redshank, and with duller leg colour. But note the flight pattern: Redshank always shows white trailing edge to the wing and white rump extending in a V up the back.

Compared with Green Sandpiper, note paler wings, especially underneath and a completely different call "chiff if if".

**Juvenile** (left) very similar to adult, slightly darker. Prefers damper, marshier habitat than does either Green or Common Sandpiper and is therefore less likely to give good views.

**Adult.** Much more likely to be seen on autumn passage than at other times of year. Readily wades in shallow water, feeding in fresh water marshes.

23 CM, 9 IN

A VERY DISTINCTIVE DUMPY, SHORT LEGGED LITTLE WADER, with a "tortoiseshell" plumage. Does not breed in Britain, but is well distributed round the coasts, even in summer. Has a very definite preference for rocky or pebbly shores, where it feeds by rummaging among seaweed. Also feeds on strand-line, turning debris to look for invertebrates. Very occasionally occurs on inland waters, but again will stick to pebbles or concrete. Note the distinctive short wedge-shaped bill and short orange legs. Non breeding plumage birds are dark greyish brown above with white on the face and underparts. They often share the same rocky places as Purple Sandpipers and look a bit like them, but note the orange (not yellow legs) and distinctive shape. Also Purple Sandpipers are much rarer winter visitors (see Purple Sandpiper, page 92). Breeding plumage Turnstone have lovely "broken" patterns of black, white and orange. You often also see sort of "in between" plumages. Turnstones call is almost impossible to write down, but is a distinctive chattering "kit it it it".

**Juvenile.** Prefers rocky shores and pebbly beaches. Feeds on insects and other invertebrates, which it finds by turning over pebbles, seaweed and debris on the tide-line.

Occurs in all sorts of mottled plumages, though **winter plumage** (above) is greyish-brown. May be seen in company with Purple Sandpiper, which likes same rocky habitat.

Does not breed in Britain, but still seen in summer on coasts. **Breeding plumage** is rich tortoiseshell pattern, of chestnut, black and white. Note orange legs and short bill.

# GREAT SKUA

## 58 CM, 23 IN

SKUAS ARE GULL-LIKE SEABIRDS, but with a faster more agile flight style, suited to their habit of harassing other birds into dropping or regurgitating their food. This is known as klepto-parasitism: translated as feeding by stealing! As the name implies, Great Skua is the largest of the Skuas. It is quite a bit bigger and bulkier than Arctic, but the difference isn't always immediately obvious with single birds. Great Skuas breed on coastal bog and moorland in the Northern Isles. They are known locally as Bonxies. Like all Skuas, they will dive bomb you if you walk through the colony – quite a frightening experience! Also occurs on seawatches in spring and autumn. Dark chocolatey brown, often with paler blotching on the head and face. Large immature gulls (Herring and Lesser Black Back ) can look almost as brown, and are about the same size, and therefore can be mistaken for Bonxies. Note the Great Skua's short wedge-shaped tail. Young gulls will also have paler upper tails and less completely dark plumage.

The bright white wing patches are conspicuous even at long range and very useful on a seawatch! Flight is heavier, steadier and less erratic than other skuas.

Only one colour phase (there's a relief!) but plumage varies. Some are dark chocolate-brown, others have almost golden tinges. Great Skuas will dive at intruders on their breeding grounds.

YOU ARE MOST LIKELY TO SEE SKUAS either in the Northern Isles, where they breed, or on a seawatch, most commonly off a headland, with an onshore wind, in spring or autumn. Four species occur in Britain, but Arctic is by far the commonest. It's not a bad rule that, if you see a skua, assume it's an Arctic until proved otherwise! Arctic Skua is smaller than a Herring Gull and clearly smaller than Great Skua (see Great Skua page 109). Birds occur in various plumages, from dark phase (can look almost black) to light phase (brown above, whitish below) and even intermediates. Juveniles are brown and barred. Pomarine and Long-tailed Skuas have similar colour phases so it's hard to separate them on plumage. Juvenile gulls and Gannets can look very dark, especially against the sun and can be mistaken for skuas. The gulls even sometimes behave like skuas, chasing other birds (see pages 120–121). As with a lot of seawatching, the trick is to get as much experience as possible, and always consider the possible confusion species.

Note elongated but fairly short central tail feathers of Arctic, compared with the streamers of Long-tailed, and the "spoons" of Pomarine.

**Juvenile** plumage is brown and barred. Arctic Skuas breed on the islands around Scotland and occur elsewhere in Britain as passage migrants.

Plumage is very variable, from dark phase to **light phase** shown here. Beware confusion with immature gulls and Gannets as well other skuas. More buoyant, graceful flight than Great Skua.

# POMARINE SKUA

## 54 CM, 21 IN

DOES NOT BREED IN BRITAIN BUT OCCURS ON MIGRATION. Often travels in quite large flocks, which are seen offshore, especially in May, off the south and east coasts, and the Outer Hebrides. Each year, new seawatching sites are tried, and new skua routes discovered. Autumn passage is less predictable, and Poms can occur from August right through to November. At all times, remember that Pom is a rarer bird than Arctic Skua. It occurs in dark and light phases, and the juveniles are barred. Adults have central tail feathers with "spoons", which are noticeable at long range, even if the impression is simply of a peculiarly elongated tail. Without the spoons, however, Pom is difficult to separate from Arctic Skua. Pom is slightly larger, rather more barrel chested and with a slightly steadier wingbeat (often likened to a large gull), but it takes experience to sort them out and sometimes even experts disagree.

Experienced seawatchers can usually make out the heavier, more barrel-chested build of Pomarine Skua compared with Arctic, but even so, wind strength and distance make it difficult.

**Juveniles** are brown and barred, difficult to separate from Arctic Skua.

Like Arctic Skua, Pomarine occurs in both a dark and a **light phase** (shown here). This is not a British breeding bird, but a passage migrant, seen off the coasts.

# COMMON GULL

THE SECOND MOST NUMEROUS OF THE SMALL GULLS. Breeds in the north of Britain, often in delightfully wild countryside, but takes to playing fields and farmland in winter. Rather less likely to visit rubbish dumps. Often in company of Black-headed Gulls. Common Gull is larger than Black-headed, but considerably smaller than the "big gulls " (Herring or Lesser Black Back). The plumage and shape, however, are rather more similar to a small Herring Gull. Amongst Black-headeds, adult Commons are distinguished by larger size, lack of head markings, slightly darker grey back, and yellowy bill and legs. The wings have black tips to the primaries, with white spots or "mirrors". No white wedge on the underwing. Young Common Gulls start brownish and then acquire a grey back, before eventually moulting into adult plumage. The call is a fairly gentle mewing. The most similar species is probably Kittiwake but Kittiwakes are exclusively birds of rocky coasts, and have black legs and solid black wing tips.

In flight, wings show black tips with white spots or "mirrors". Young birds (as above right) gradually become greyer through the second winter (above left) to the winter adult (above) which has just a streaked head.

**Young** Common Gull (left). Brownish then acquires grey back. before eventually moulting into adult plumage. Bill and legs are pinkish or greyish-pink and the bill often has a blackish tip.

Larger than Black-headed, the **adult** Common Gull looks rather like a small Herring Gull, but has more gentle expression. Common has yellow bill and legs.

# KITTIWAKE
### 41 CM, 16 IN

A SMALL GULL THAT LOOKS RATHER SIMILAR TO A COMMON GULL, but has very different habits and habitat preference. Kittiwakes breed on sea cliffs – often in very large colonies – and winter largely out to sea. Very rarely recorded inland, usually only when storm driven. Even at the coast, they seem loath to get away from rocks or jetties; some even nest on quayside buildings. A common sight on a seawatch, so need to be distinguished from Common Gull. Note wing pattern. Adult Kittiwake has a solid dipped-in-ink black wing tip: a feature surprisingly easy to appreciate even at long range. Juvenile Kittiwakes have a very distinctive black W pattern on their upperwings, and a black half collar on the hind neck, and a black tail band. This plumage is similar to Little Gull, but Kittiwake is clearly larger and with a less fluttery flight. Kittiwakes very obligingly remind us of their name by calling: "kitti wake kitti wake".

Compared with Common Gull, note solid inky black wing tip. **Juvenile** (below right) has black W pattern on upperwings, black half collar and black tail band.

Breeds in large colonies on seacliffs. At closer range or at rest, note that the bill is yellow but the feet are black (greeny yellow in Common Gull).

# BLACK-HEADED GULL

## 35–38 CM, 14–15 IN

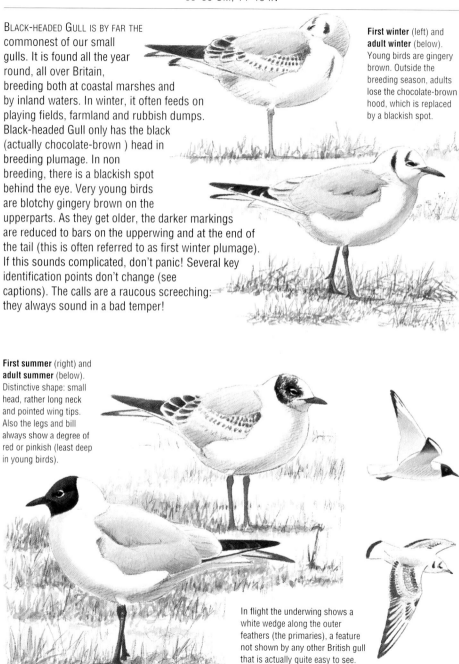

BLACK-HEADED GULL IS BY FAR THE commonest of our small gulls. It is found all the year round, all over Britain, breeding both at coastal marshes and by inland waters. In winter, it often feeds on playing fields, farmland and rubbish dumps. Black-headed Gull only has the black (actually chocolate-brown ) head in breeding plumage. In non breeding, there is a blackish spot behind the eye. Very young birds are blotchy gingery brown on the upperparts. As they get older, the darker markings are reduced to bars on the upperwing and at the end of the tail (this is often referred to as first winter plumage). If this sounds complicated, don't panic! Several key identification points don't change (see captions). The calls are a raucous screeching: they always sound in a bad temper!

**First winter** (left) and **adult winter** (below). Young birds are gingery brown. Outside the breeding season, adults lose the chocolate-brown hood, which is replaced by a blackish spot.

**First summer** (right) and **adult summer** (below). Distinctive shape: small head, rather long neck and pointed wing tips. Also the legs and bill always show a degree of red or pinkish (least deep in young birds).

In flight the underwing shows a white wedge along the outer feathers (the primaries), a feature not shown by any other British gull that is actually quite easy to see.

THE FIRST STEP IN GULL IDENTIFICATION is to separate the various species into small and large gulls. The second step is to get to know the commonest species, and compare others with them. The third key to gull identification is to realize that all gulls have several plumages which can look very different: breeding, non breeding and various stages of juvenile plumage, for gulls may take several years to reach maturity. The Mediterranean Gull, though rare, is always worth keeping your eyes peeled for at a gull roost. Although it breeds in extremely small numbers, it is slightly more common in winter and young birds may be seen in late spring. Compare with both Black-headed (with which this species occasionally breeds) and Common Gull. Note adult has no black on wings, and white forewing rather than pale leading edge of Black-headed. Red bill and long red legs. In winter plumage, very pale with "pirate's patch" smudging eye. In flight has shallower wingbeats than Common Gull.

**Adult in summer** (above) has black hood, more extensive than Black-headed Gull. Note pale forewing – no black tips to primaries. **Second-year birds** (right and far right), however, do show black wing tips. They are most likely to be confused with juvenile Common gull.

Compare **juvenile** (foreground) with **adult** at rear. Note patch over eye.

# LITTLE GULL
## 28 CM, 11 IN

As the name implies, the smallest British gull. It looks rather like a tiny Black-headed Gull, but is much rarer. Little Gulls do not breed in Britain, but there is a large population in Holland, which pass along our east coast in spring and autumn, sometimes in quite large numbers. East winds may drift flocks well inland to reservoirs or lakes. There are also wintering flocks in one or two favoured locations in the Irish sea. Nevertheless, it is quite possible to pass a year's birding in Britain without seeing a Little Gull! Breeding plumage adults have a completely black hood, white wing tips, but a rather unexpected dusky grey underwing. In non breeding plumage, the hood is reduced to a black cap and a black spot behind the eye. Juveniles – the likeliest plumage in autumn – have blackish backs and caps and a dark W marking across the wings. This plumage is very similar to juvenile Kittiwake (see Kittiwake, page 113) but Kittiwakes are very rare away from the sea.

In flight, **juvenile** (right) shows dark W across wings, like Kittiwake. Look for the darker back (mantle) of Little Gull and the fluttery flight. **Breeding plumage adult** (far right) shows dark underwing.

**Juvenile** (below) has blackish cap and spot behind the eye. In **intermediate plumages** (left) birds show fewer black markings than juveniles.

**Adult in breeding plumage** (left) looks like a tiny Black-headed Gull. Little Gulls do not breed in Britain, although they do in Holland. They winter at sea.

# HERRING GULL

56–66 CM, 22–26 IN

THE MOST WIDESPREAD OF THE BIG GULLS. Nests all round the coast, often in large colonies, and winters everywhere, including inland on fields and rubbish dumps. Large roosts occur on reservoirs and lakes. Although the plumage is not dissimilar to Common Gull, Herring is much bigger. Adults have grey back, white underparts, and black wing tips, with white spots or "mirrors". Note leg colour is pinkish. Most similar species is Lesser Black-backed Gull (see page 118), which has a darker back (but not actually black!) and yellow legs. Juvenile large gulls are less easy to identify. Any flock of large gulls is likely to have birds in various plumages, so it's important to appreciate the typical size and jizz of any one species. Herring Gull is a little larger than Lesser Black-back, but clearly smaller than Great Black-back. Juvenile plumages tend to be less dark than either of the Black-backs. Call: the familiar seagull cry.

**Juvenile** in flight has darker forewing, dark tail band. Note white spots or "mirrors" on adult's wing tips. Strong flyer, with much soaring and gliding.

**Adult** (top). Larger than Lesser Black-back; grey back, yellow bill and eye and pinkish legs. Black wing tips with white spots.

Really young Herring Gulls are blotchy brown, with blackish wing markings and tail band. Then, at the **intermediate plumage** stage (above), the greyer feathers begin to appear, firstly on the back.

**Juvenile.** Herring Gulls take four years to reach maturity, and become gradually greyer throughout this period until they attain full adult plumage.

117

# LESSER BLACK-BACKED GULL

## 53–56 CM, 21–22 IN

MOST NUMEROUS DURING THE SUMMER, when it breeds on northern coasts and even inland moorlands, most commonly in north of Britain, but is spreading. Increasingly present during the winter months, in similar habitats to Herring Gull. Adults distinguished from Herring Gull by darker back (mantle). Some of them (Scandinavian race) are almost black, but others are merely dark grey, but always darker than Herring Gull. Lesser Black-back also has yellow legs (pink in Herring). Juveniles have the same range of plumages as Herring Gull, taking four years to become fully adult, but Lesser Black-back is generally rather darker, especially on the wings. Lesser Black-back is a little smaller and slimmer than Herring Gull, but this isn't always easy to appreciate unless the species are together. To separate from Great Black-back: Lesser is considerably smaller, Great has blacker back, but with more white patches, and has pink legs. Juveniles have whiter heads (see Great Black-back). Call: similar to Herring Gull.

**Adult** Lesser Black-back (below) has yellow bill, eyes and legs. Depth of colour on the back variable from almost black to dark grey, depending on race.

Occurs throughout the year, in similar habitats as Herring Gull, but may breed near inland waters.

Like Herring Gull, Lesser Black-backs take four years to reach maturity, and their plumage gradually changes from brown to **adult's** dark grey and white (above).

**Juveniles** tend to be darker than young Herring Gulls, especially on the wings, but this is variable and sometimes immature birds of the two species are indistinguishable in the field.

# GREAT BLACK-BACKED GULL
## 64–79 CM, 25–31 IN

AS THE NAME IMPLIES, LARGER – CONSIDERABLY SO – THAN LESSER BLACK-BACK. Adults have really black backs, but have more white flecks on the closed wing. Bill and eyes are yellow, but the legs are pink (yellow in Lesser). Juveniles have whiter heads than Lesser or Herring and bolder black and white chequered upperparts. Great Black-backs breed on rocky coasts, cliffs and islands, but rarely in such large colonies as the other big gulls. They winter on estuaries and marshes, but are much scarcer inland. A Black-backed gull inland is much more likely to be a Lesser. The call has a deep almost goose-like quality.

Much more exclusively coastal than the other large gulls. **Adult** (below and far right) is darker than Lesser Black-back.

Great Black-backs feed on a wide variety of animals, they can be seen hawking for flying ants or prowling puffin colonies for both young and unwary adult birds.

Compare whiter head and underparts of **immature birds** (above and left) with Lesser Black-backed and Herring Gulls.

FINAL WARNING NOTE ON BIG GULLS. In flight, especially going to roost or on migration, flocks often fly in V formation. At a distance, they can easily be mistaken for geese! A proper scrutiny will soon reveal their longer, slimmer wings, and obvious beaks.

# SIMILAR SPECIES:
# SEABIRDS IN FLIGHT

ON A SEAWATCH, BIRDS ARE OFTEN SEEN AT A DISTANCE OR AGAINST THE LIGHT, thus making identification tricky. It is a good rule that if you think you may have spotted one of the scarcer seabirds – a skua or a shearwater – just check that it isn't a more common species.

Juvenile Lesser Black-backed Gulls are typical impersonators of Arctic Skuas, particularly when silhouetted against the sun. Gannet in dark juvenile plumage is another Skua impersonator.

Juvenile Lesser Black-backed Gull

Adult Great Black-backed Gull

Juvenile Gannet

Adult Arctic Skua

Fulmar

Guillemot

Sooty Shearwater

Manx Shearwater

A lot of seabirds look basically dark above and white below. Both shearwaters and Fulmar fly with a stiff-winged gliding style, while auks (Guillemots etc) fly on fast whirring wings.

Seabird plumages vary considerably with age (and indeed with the effects of the light and at long distance) and Skuas even come in various different "phases", so "jizz" is all important.

Adult Great Black-backed Gull

Adult Lesser Black-backed Gull

Adult dark phase Pomarine Skua

Juvenile Arctic Skua

Juvenile Lesser Black-backed Gull

Juvenile Gannet

Juvenile Herring Gull

2nd year Gannet

Great Skua

Pale immature Pomarine Skua

Note the flight styles: are wings stiff (like a glider – or shearwater) or flappy (like a gull or skua)? Some birds – like Gannets – do a bit of both!

TERNS ARE SMALLER AND MORE SLENDER THAN GULLS, with slimmer wings and a faster flight style that often involves hovering or skimming over the water when feeding. They are all summer visitors to Britain, arriving in April or May and very rarely seen after late September or early October. Size, bill and leg colour are important when separating the species. Common Terns breed round the coast, often in colonies, and also increasingly on inland waters, often on specially provided rafts. It's not a bad rule to assume that a "white" tern inland is most likely to be a Common. Like other tern species, it has a black cap. In late autumn the forehead becomes whiter; the bill and legs darker. (See also Roseate Tern, opposite). Common *is* commonest, except in the north of Britain, where Arctic Tern takes over. Inland, Arctics occur on passage, but are nothing like as frequent as Common. Roseate is rare, usually seen in a few favoured locations only. Common Tern's call is a harsh "skeee ar" or a short "ki kik".

The best feature in flight is a dark wedge on the upperwing, on the outer primary feathers, which Arctic lacks.

**Adult in non breeding plumage** (right) in late autumn. The forehead goes whiter and the bill and legs darker.

**Juvenile.** White forehead and dark wing markings. Juvenile and non breeding Common and Arctic are hard to separate. Birders often refer to Commic Terns!

In **breeding plumage,** the bill is scarlet with a black tip, and the legs are also scarlet. The very similar Arctic Tern has a deeper blood red bill and legs.

# ARCTIC TERN
### 35 CM, 14 IN

ARCTIC TERN BREEDS ON THE COAST (and occasionally inland ) in the north of Britain, where Common becomes scarcer. Arctics are usually in larger colonies. They occur on inland waters on passage, particularly in spring. Looks very similar to Common Tern. The calls are very similar to Common Tern: "kee ar" and "kik kik". The champion migrant, some birds breed in the Arctic and winter in the Antarctic.

**Adult** lacks a dark primary wedge on upperwing. **Juveniles** similar to Common Tern, but the trailing edge to upperwing is cleaner white.

**Juvenile.**

Very similar to Common Tern, but in **breeding plumage,** the bill is dark blood red and has no black tip. Slightly shorter legs, also dark red; generally has longer tail streamers.

# ROSEATE TERN
### 38 CM, 15 IN

THE RAREST OF THE MEDIUM-SIZED "WHITE" TERNS. Breeds in a very few well known and well protected sites. In breeding plumage looks similar to Common (and Arctic) Terns, but is brighter white, especially on upper wings and is slightly larger and more slender, with longer tail streamers. The call is a distinctive rasping sound, sometimes likened to a tarpaulin being torn!

**Juveniles** (behind) look more black and white than the other young terns, with stronger black chequering on the back, and with black legs and fuller black cap.

**Breeding plumage** (foreground). Bill is almost black, just a flush of red at the base. Legs are red. The breast sometimes shows a pinkish (roseate) flush.

# SANDWICH TERN

42 CM, 16.5 IN

THE LARGEST OF THE "WHITE", BLACK-CAPPED TERNS. Clearly bigger than Common, Arctic, or Roseate, with long thin wings, less deeply forked tail and a shaggy crest. Adults have black bill with a yellow tip and black legs. Non breeding and juveniles have white forehead, and very young birds have black chequering on the back. The call is a harsh "kirrick" (clearly different from the other terns). The youngsters also give a thin squeaking, especially heard in autumn. Sandwich Terns arrive earlier than the other species and stay later, very occasionally even wintering. They are very much coastal birds, though they prefer sandy or grassy – rather than rocky – breeding areas. They are very unusual on inland waters, though sometimes come through on passage. Flying past on a seawatch, their whiteness may recall Roseate Tern, but Sandwich is clearly larger and slimmer – and much commoner! When diving to feed, plunges from a greater height than other terns.

Whiter and longer, thinner wings than other terns.
Flight a little heavier and less buoyant than other terns.

**Adult breeding plumage** (right).
Shaggy crest, black bill with yellow
tip – easy!

**Juvenile.** Frequently gives a thin,
rather pathetic squeaky call.

# LITTLE TERN
24 CM, 9.5 IN

BY FAR THE SMALLEST OF THE BLACK-CAPPED "WHITE" TERNS, with a very fast flapping flight style, involving much hovering and plunge diving when feeding. They tend to feed in shallower water than other tern species, often at the breakwater. The forehead is white in all plumages. In breeding plumage, the bill is bright yellow with a black tip, and legs are yellow. Bill and legs are duller in juveniles, which also have brown markings on the back and upperwings. The call is a high-pitched "kik ki kik". All in all, not a difficult bird to identify. Little Terns breed round the coasts of Britain, nesting in shallow scrapes but their preference for sandy or shingly beaches makes them very vulnerable to human disturbance, and their numbers are decreasing where they are not fully protected. They are very scarce on inland waters. Like Sandwich Terns they fly out to West Africa for the winter. Young birds take two years to reach maturity and return to their place of birth.

Flying with fast, flickering wingbeats, Little Terns feed with much hovering and plunge diving, often into waves breaking close to the shore.

Winter type plumage (left) – very rarely seen in Britain. Juvenile (below) – don't worry too much about plumage details. Their small size makes them pretty unmistakable.

Adult breeding plumage. Neat white forehead, yellow bill, tiny size – nothing else like it.

# BLACK TERN
## 24 CM, 9.5 IN

BELONGS TO THE GROUP KNOWN AS "MARSH TERNS". Black Terns breed as close as Holland but have not nested regularly in Britain since the last century. They are, fairly common on passage, particularly in late April and May, over inland lakes and marshes by the coast, and sometimes offshore with other seabirds. Juveniles and non breeding adults can be puzzling. Compared with Common or Arctic Tern, Black Tern is smaller, with darker grey upperparts, dark rump, short almost square-ended tail, and a small black half collar on the shoulder. This plumage is a little reminiscent of some Little Gull plumages (see Little Gull, page 116) but juvenile Little Gulls have a striking black W on the upperwing, while non breeding adults have paler upperwings than Black Terns. Adult Black Terns coming out of breeding plumage (usually seen in July or early August) can look very blotchy, with patches of black and white on their bodies. When feeding they skim and dip to take food off the water surface. Call: a soft "kik kik".

Flight when feeding has dipping, skimming, swallow-like quality. Can turn up on passage, especially in April and May. The key to their appearance at such times is the onset of an easterly wind, particularly with thundery weather. They may often be in the company of Little Gulls.

In **breeding plumage** (left), Black Tern lives up to its name: it is sooty black on the body, greyer on the wings, with white undertail. **Moulting birds** (above) can be puzzling.

**Juvenile.** Compare with Common and Arctic Terns and also with Little Gull.

SUMMER ADULTS

Sandwich Tern

Common Tern

Little Tern

TERNS ARE ALWAYS MORE BUOYANT and slender-winged than even Kittiwakes and Little Gulls. Flight identification of terns is tricky, especially in juvenile plumage. Note the wing markings of the various species.

Little Gull

Arctic Tern

Kittiwake

Roseate Tern

JUVENILE PLUMAGE

Black Tern

Arctic Tern

Sandwich Tern

Little Tern

Roseate Tern

1st winter Little Gull

Common Tern

Kittiwake

ADULT WINTER/LATE AUTUMN

Common Tern

Sandwich Tern

Little Gull

Arctic Tern

# GUILLEMOT

## 42 CM, 16.5 IN

BELONGS TO THE FAMILY KNOWN AS AUKS (the northern hemisphere equivalent of penguins, except that they can fly!). Widespread, breeding round the coasts on steep rocky cliff ledges, sometimes in very large colonies. The other common British auks are Razorbill and Puffin. All are easy to identify at close quarters. Note Guillemot's browner plumage and thin pointed beak. Some have white "spectacles" and are known as "bridled". However, when seen flying by on a seawatch, or at a distance on the sea, auks are not so easy to identify. Birders often resort to noting them simply as "auks sp." -meaning they are not sure! With practice, you can notice the Guillemot's more cigar-shaped body and browner plumage. In winter plumage, the face becomes whiter. Distant birds on the water could be mistaken for small seaducks or even grebes (see page 21). Auks spend much of their winter way out in the ocean, and are much less numerous round our coasts than in the breeding season or on passage.

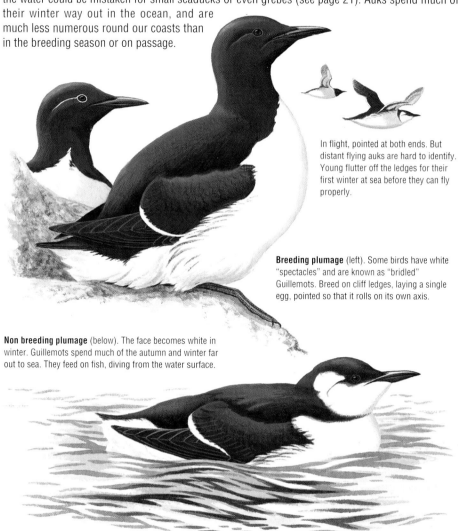

In flight, pointed at both ends. But distant flying auks are hard to identify. Young flutter off the ledges for their first winter at sea before they can fly properly.

**Breeding plumage** (left). Some birds have white "spectacles" and are known as "bridled" Guillemots. Breed on cliff ledges, laying a single egg, pointed so that it rolls on its own axis.

**Non breeding plumage** (below). The face becomes white in winter. Guillemots spend much of the autumn and winter far out to sea. They feed on fish, diving from the water surface.

# RAZORBILL

SIMILAR HABITS AND SIMILAR PLUMAGE TO GUILLEMOT, but generally not quite so numerous round our coasts, though we do have a large percentage of the world's population breeding in Britain, on rocky cliffs. They favour less exposed places than the Guillemots, preferring to nest in crevices rather than ledges. The plumage is blacker than Guillemot's, and the bill is a deep (old-fashioned razor) shape, with white bands on it, and with a white eyestreak above. The bill is, however, not so parrot-like as Puffin. Puffin also has a white face. Razorbills tend to swim with their tails cocked and they look a little stockier than Guillemot. At distance, or in flight, usually looks blacker than Guillemot, and with less pointed ends. The face becomes white in winter and – like other auks – they can be mistaken for seaducks on the water, at a distance (see page 21).Young birds have smaller bills, and like young Guillemots, launch themselves off the cliff-face before they can fly properly, to winter at sea with the parent birds.

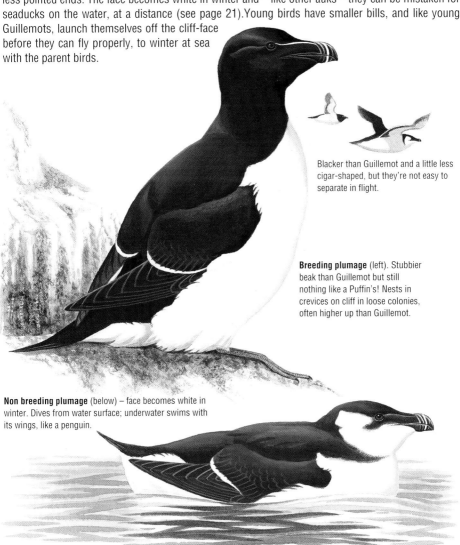

Blacker than Guillemot and a little less cigar-shaped, but they're not easy to separate in flight.

**Breeding plumage** (left). Stubbier beak than Guillemot but still nothing like a Puffin's! Nests in crevices on cliff in loose colonies, often higher up than Guillemot.

**Non breeding plumage** (below) – face becomes white in winter. Dives from water surface; underwater swims with its wings, like a penguin.

# BLACK GUILLEMOT

## 34 CM, 13.5 IN

Often called Tystie (its old Norse name). Breeds on rocky coasts, mainly in the north of Britain and in Ireland. Nests in crevices and caves, and is not as obviously colonial as the other auks. Similar shape to a Guillemot (pointed beak) but considerably smaller. Breeding plumage is very distinctive – velvety black, with red feet and inside to the mouth, and with a bright white wing patch. Winter and juvenile plumage is quite different: messily whitish, with variable dark grey on head, back and flanks. This resembles some plumages of Long-tailed Duck, especially if the bird is diving on the sea at a distance! Theoretically, the breeding plumage is not dissimilar to male Velvet Scoter (see page 47) but Scoters are much bigger, and have white head markings, and in fact the white wing patch is on the speculum. Black Guillemot is rarely involved in seabird movements like the other auks, and is scarce in southern waters.

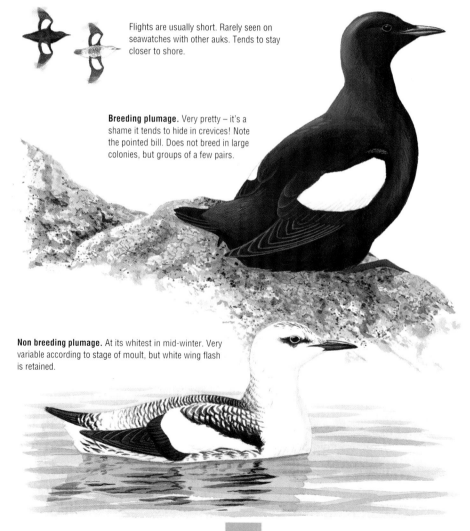

Flights are usually short. Rarely seen on seawatches with other auks. Tends to stay closer to shore.

**Breeding plumage.** Very pretty – it's a shame it tends to hide in crevices! Note the pointed bill. Does not breed in large colonies, but groups of a few pairs.

**Non breeding plumage.** At its whitest in mid-winter. Very variable according to stage of moult, but white wing flash is retained.

# PUFFIN
### 30 CM, 12 IN

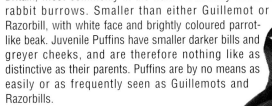

ONE OF BRITAIN'S BEST LOVED AND MOST RECOGNIZABLE BIRDS. Breeds on the coast and on islands round Britain, most commonly in the north. It actually nests in deep crevices or underground, often in rabbit burrows. Smaller than either Guillemot or Razorbill, with white face and brightly coloured parrot-like beak. Juvenile Puffins have smaller darker bills and greyer cheeks, and are therefore nothing like as distinctive as their parents. Puffins are by no means as easily or as frequently seen as Guillemots and Razorbills.

Flying by out to sea, or on the water, the small size and white face is still noticeable. Most confusable with Little Auk. Rarely seen in large numbers on seawatch.

Look for Puffins on clifftops, where they nest under boulders or in rabbit burrows. **Adult** (above right) is unmistakable. **Juvenile** (above) has smaller bill and greyer cheeks than breeding adult.

# LITTLE AUK
### 20 CM, 8 IN

VERY SMALL INDEED. STARLING SIZED. Dumpy, black above, white below, with very fast whirring wings. Little Auks occasionally occur in large numbers, mainly off the east coast in November, and sometimes other winter months. At such times, flocks may be seen racing past offshore, or even tagging along with Starlings! Birds are sometimes "wrecked" inland, and have been known to drop onto small ponds or even down into city streets. These movements are clearly triggered by certain weather patterns or food shortages, but we don't know exactly why or when they will occur.

At a distance flocks look rather like small black and white waders! Single bird resembles a small, fast Puffin with no visible bill.

It is possible to go for years without seeing a Little Auk then – if you get lucky on a seawatch – you may see hundreds!

# FERAL PIGEON

## 33 CM, 13 IN

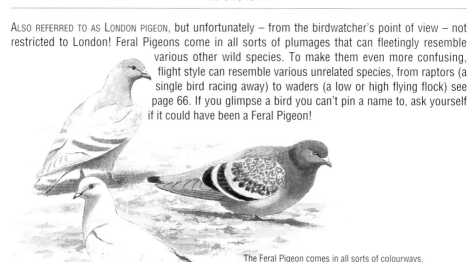

ALSO REFERRED TO AS LONDON PIGEON, but unfortunately – from the birdwatcher's point of view – not restricted to London! Feral Pigeons come in all sorts of plumages that can fleetingly resemble various other wild species. To make them even more confusing, flight style can resemble various unrelated species, from raptors (a single bird racing away) to waders (a low or high flying flock) see page 66. If you glimpse a bird you can't pin a name to, ask yourself if it could have been a Feral Pigeon!

The Feral Pigeon comes in all sorts of colourways, including one that is identical to its wild ancestor, the Rock Dove (see page 230). In flight, it can be mistaken for other species.

# STOCK DOVE

## 33 CM, 13 IN

BREEDS IN MOST PARTS OF BRITAIN, EXCEPT IN THE FAR NORTH. Nests in holes in trees in park or farmland. Never as numerous as the Wood Pigeon, though it may feed with it in mixed flocks. Smaller than Wood Pigeon, lacks white on the neck or in the wing and has a dark eye. The call is a soft "oo woo", which is rather owl-like, quite different from the more expected cooing of a pigeon.

Similar to Rock Dove (or Rock Dove type feral pigeons) but has only short thin black wings bars, and dark rump. In flight has black trailing edge to wings and tail.

# WOOD PIGEON
### 41 CM, 16 IN

THE LARGEST OF OUR PIGEONS. Common in all sorts of habitats all over the country, though understandably scarcer on some remote and generally treeless islands. Often gathers in large flocks in winter, especially on farmland, and large movements occur in the autumn, probably involving continental birds. Distinguished from Stock Dove or Feral (Rock Dove type) Pigeon by large size, bright white mark on the neck, and white wing flashes when it flies (often noticeable even at rest). Juveniles lack the white neck patches, but still have the white on the wings). "Claps" its wings noisily when disturbed as it panics away. It also claps during its display flight, which involves soaring up high then gliding down wih wings held in a V shape. The call is an insistent and rhythmic "coo coo-cooo", which is relaxing or annoying, depending on your taste! Nests in trees, where it builds an untidy and flimsy platform of twigs. Feeds mostly on vegetable matter, including cereal crops, seeds and berries.

**Juvenile.** Wood Pigeons usually lay two eggs, and like other members of the pigeon family, rear their young on a substance, called pigeon's milk, which is made in the adult's crops.

White crescents on wings obvious. Wood Pigeons make loud clapping noise when flushed and will also clap in display flight.

**Adult.** Close views – and birds in town parks are a lot tamer than their country cousins! – reveal the pinkish breast, and glossy metallic sheen to the sides of neck.

# COLLARED DOVE

## 32 CM, 12.5 IN

ALTHOUGH THE FIRST COLLARED DOVES ONLY ARRIVED IN BRITAIN IN THE MID-1950S, the species has spread to most parts of the country, to the extent that these birds are now almost as familiar as Wood Pigeons in some areas. Particularly fond of farmyards, the Collared Dove also breeds in gardens and parkland. Its rapid expansion in range has partly been attributed to its very long breeding season – from February to October in Britain. Slimmer and longer tailed than any of the pigeons, the Collared Dove is basically similar to the Turtle Dove, but Collared is seen all the year round (Turtle Dove is a summer visitor) and the plumage looks much smoother. Fawn above and pale grey below, with a thin black collar. More like Turtle Dove in flight, but note Collared's plainer back and wings, with only the wing tips dark, and paler tail. Both Collared and Turtle Doves have white edges to the tail when seen from above. The call is a monotonous "koo kookok", and a rather whingey nasal "kwerr".

In flight similar to Turtle Dove, but note plainer back and wings. Has broader, but less bright white tail band than Turtle Dove.

Collared Doves often choose dense conifer trees to nest in. They usually have two broods per year, but as many as five have been attempted!

**Juvenile** birds are greyer on the back, with a less well developed half collar.

# TURTLE DOVE
## 27 CM, 11 IN

THE OTHER SMALL DOVE IN BRITAIN. A summer visitor only, and in sadly decreasing numbers. Arrives late April or May. More often heard than seen. The call is a lovely gentle purring. If seen in flight, it has a very fast style, with an even quicker flap than Collared Dove. The scaly feathering on the back and wings, darker trailing edge to the wing, bright white undertail and black tail centre all give it a less bland look than Collared Dove. Seen at rest, the plumage has a lovely pale chestnut warmth to it, and there is a black and white neck patch. Like Collared Dove, it shows white outer tail when seen from above, but the centre of the tail is black. Commonest in south and eastern Britain, quite scarce in Scotland and Ireland. Although it nests deep in trees or hedges, migrants may occur at the coast in more open habitat, such as stubble fields.

Fast in flight. Spangled back; white edges and dark centre to tail give diamond shape when taking off from the ground. More contrasting white undertail than Collared Dove.

**Juvenile** similar to **adult** (pair above), but slightly paler and greyer and without neck bars. Found mostly in the south and east of England; feeds mainly on weed seeds.

# CUCKOO

EVERYONE KNOWS THE CALL and is aware of its habit of laying eggs in other birds' nests, but this is a surprisingly hard species to actually see. Cuckoos are purely summer visitors, arriving in mid-April and usually gone before the end of September. You are most likely to see one in flight, especially as it crosses open habitat, such as reedbed. One of the Cuckoo's favourite host species is Reed Warbler. Notice the longer tapering tail, and the droopy-winged look. The barred underparts are similar to a Sparrowhawk (see page 58). Adults are grey, but juveniles are rich brown, with a white spot on the back of the neck. There is also a very rare brown adult phase. As well as the familiar "cuckoo", females also have a strange bubbling call, sometimes heard in spring. They feed on insects and particularly hairy caterpillars, so they also spend time on the ground.

The flight is fast and shallow-winged and this – coupled with the slim build and long tail – gives it a rather hawk-like jizz.

**Females** (left) will lay in several nests over the course of several days. Often mobbed by small birds.

**Adult male** (top) is grey as is grey-phase female; **juveniles** (left) are rich brown with a white patch on the nape.

# BARN OWL
### 34 CM, 13.5 IN

ALTHOUGH, LIKE ALL OWLS, BARN OWLS ARE LARGELY NOCTURNAL, they also hunt at dawn and dusk, sometimes until the sun is well up. In flight, they look a ghostly white, although in fact the back is a sort of gentle honey colour. The face is more oval-shaped than other owls. They hunt over fields and along roadsides, which means your best chance of seeing them is often from a car. It also means that – sadly – many of them end up as road kills. The only other white-looking owl is the very rare Snowy Owl, which is much bigger and seen only occasionally in Scotland or the Northern Isles. Barn Owls do not hoot in any way: they produce various eerie shrieks, as well as hissing and snoring noises. They breed in hollow trees, old barns and – increasingly – in specially provided nesting boxes. Found in most parts of Britain and Ireland, but scarce in northern Scotland.

Feeds almost entirely on small mammals such as voles and rats, and small birds. Hunts low over fields. Wing feathers are fringed, which enables it to fly silently.

Distinctive heart-shaped face, white underparts and long legs – the Barn Owl is pretty unmistakable. Seen at dusk it is a ghostly white, big-headed bird.

# LITTLE OWL

## 22 CM, 8.5 IN

WIDESPREAD IN BRITAIN (EXCEPT IRELAND) but perhaps becoming scarcer. Not a true native, it was introduced from the 1840s onwards with the object of reducing garden pests; it feeds on insects, small mammals and birds. Little Owls often roost during the day in surprisingly conspicuous places, such as on barn roofs, walls, cliffs or bare trees, and they sometimes draw attention to themselves by calling. They give a rather mewing repeated "kee u kee u". They really are little – barely half the size of a Tawny – and the most obvious feature is the face pattern of whitish eyebrows and chinstrap, and piercing yellow eyes. They often bob when alarmed. The flight is a fast flap and glide, often close to the ground, before they swoop back up onto a perch. Probably the best place to look for them is established hedgerows with gnarled – or even dead – tree trunks in them. They are also fond of quarries. They nest mainly in tree holes, but will also take to specially provided nest boxes.

Fast flapping flight, and glide, close to ground, before swooping back to perch.

The Little Owl can sit still for hours, a round ball of fluff, but if alarmed, it can suddenly go very thin as it stretches upwards.

White eyebrows and piercing yellow eyes give this tiny owl a fierce expression. Look for it at dusk in hedgerows and by the sides of country roads.

# TAWNY OWL

## 38 CM, 15 IN

ARGUABLY THE MOST WIDESPREAD OF THE BRITISH OWLS (although it is absent from Ireland) but one of the most difficult to see. By day, Tawny Owls roost in holes or in trees, when their presence may be betrayed by the noise of small birds mobbing them. Even then it may be hard to spot the owl unless it flies and, even when it does, it will soon glide away into the woods and be lost again. Otherwise, you may see the silhouette of a bird at night when it is out hunting. It will rarely be far from woods with mature trees. Tawny Owl is basically brown and streaky. It shares this type of plumage with several other species, but Tawny is considerably larger than Little Owl and would rarely be seen in open country like Short-eared. It is most likely to be confused with Long-eared (see page 140). Tawny is plumper, rounder faced and lacks any ear tufts. The call is the familiar "hoo hoo hooo", and a sharp "keewick".

A woodland bird and very nocturnal in its habits, the Tawny Owl is much more likely to be heard than seen. Feeds mainly on small mammals such as wood mice.

By day the Tawny Owl roosts, often hunched against a tree-trunk, when despite its camouflage, its presence may be advertised by small birds mobbing it.

**Juvenile** (right). Nests in holes in trees. When still by no means fully fledged, the young may start to scramble about among the branches.

# LONG-EARED OWL

NOT AN EASY BIRD TO SEE, although it breeds quite widely throughout Britain, mainly in conifer plantations. The commonest Owl in Ireland (where it is also found in deciduous woods). Very secretive during the breeding season, but you may hear its low long hoot, or the high-pitched "squeaky gate" calls of youngsters. Your best chance of seeing Long-eared Owl is if you visit a winter roost. This may be in quite open bramble or bushes, and may contain up to a dozen birds, which sit beautifully camouflaged, defying you to count them. These are probably immigrants from the continent, and in late autumn they sometimes arrive on the coasts along with Short-eared Owls. The ear tufts are only visible if you get a good view of a bird at rest, but they are then clearly much longer than those of Short-eared. Tawny Owl (page 138) is plumper and rounder faced, has no ear tufts at all, and has darker eyes, compared to the bright orange of Long-eared.

Generally most day-flying large brown owls will be Short-eared. Long-eared tends to roost by day, exquisitely camouflaged beside a tree trunk.

Compared with Short-eared, note more extensive streaking on the underparts (breast only on Short-eared) and slightly more rufous patches on upperwing. Longer and slimmer than Tawny Owl.

# SHORT-EARED OWL
## 38 CM; 15 IN

QUITE COMMONLY HUNTS DURING DAYLIGHT, so it's a good rule that any day hunting large brown owl is likely to be Short-eared. Quarters open country, flapping and gliding with wings held in a shallow V, at a distance, very reminiscent of a harrier and – since female and juvenile harriers are also largely brown – look for the ring tail and slimmer build of Hen and Montagu's (see pages 56 and 57). Breeds in moorland and young plantations in northern Britain, but you are most likely to see Short-eared Owls on passage in late autumn, or at their wintering places, flat rough ground or marsh land. In flight, very similar to Long-eared, but streaking on the underparts is across the breast only, and contrasts with the whiter belly and flanks. The upperwing has yellowy – rather than rufous – wing patches, but this is variable and hard to see. Often perches on the ground or on very low stumps or tussocks. Song – only heard in its northern breeding haunts – is a hollow "boo boo boo boo".

Compared with Long-eared the streaking on the underparts is across the breast only and contrasts with the whiter belly and flanks. Upperwing has yellowy rather than rufous patches.

At rest, the face is rounder than Long-eared, eyes yellower and ear tufts almost invisible.

# NIGHTJAR
## 27 CM, 10.5 IN

EXTREMELY DIFFICULT TO SEE. A summer visitor (arriving in mid-May and rarely seen after the breeding season). Breeds on heathlands and low plantations, mainly in the south and east of England. You are not likely to find a Nightjar unless you visit one of its known sites, preferably in late May or early June. Then wait until dusk, when the birds will begin churring – the noise sounds rather like a distant motor scooter! Look towards the lightest part of the sky and hope that the bird flies through it, chasing insects, giving a soft sharp "too wick" call. You may see white flashes on the wing tips and tail end, but generally the plumage is as dense as "dead leaves". Although Nightjars are long-distance migrants (they winter in Africa) they are very rarely seen on passage. Perhaps the species most often misidentified as Nightjar is Mistle Thrush, especially the speckly young birds, which also have white tail edges, and a rattling call. However, Mistle Thrushes are much commoner and only fly by day!

Flight shape is slim, long-winged and long-tailed and acrobatic – very much like an agile, nocturnal falcon. Male shows most conspicuous white flashes on wing tips and tail end.

Plumage as dense as "dead leaves". This is precisely why the bird is so utterly camouflaged on the ground on its nest, or roosting along a tree branch.

# KINGFISHER

16.5 CM, 6.5 IN

Arguably Britain's most beautiful and most easily recognized bird. Found near lakes, rivers and canals, all over Britain, except Scotland, where it is restricted to the south. Seen perched, it is unmistakable, but it is perhaps more often seen flashing past and disappearing round a corner. In flight, it can look either metallic blue or bright orange, depending which side catches the light. The call is a short "peep peep", and it is often this noise that attracts attention before you actually see the bird. Once perched in cover alongside water, Kingfishers can be very hard to spot, despite their brilliant colours. The best technique is often to scan along likely looking perches with binoculars. Kingfishers nest deep in tunnels, excavated into a sandy river bank. The female has a reddish base to the beak. In winter, birds may move to coastal estuaries, and they are sometimes even seen on rocks or breakwaters at the seaside. Kingfishers hunt for food by diving, usually from a perch, but may hover briefly. Prey is swallowed head first.

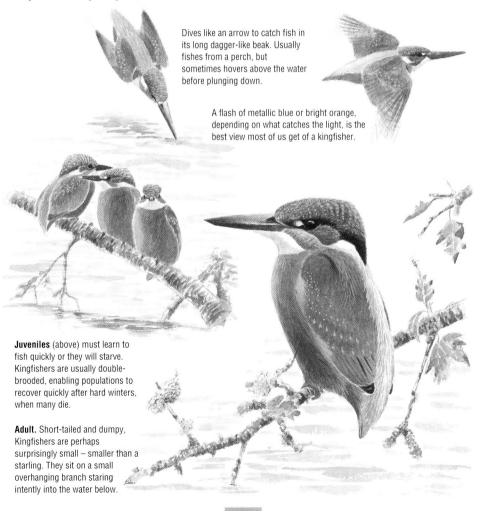

Dives like an arrow to catch fish in its long dagger-like beak. Usually fishes from a perch, but sometimes hovers above the water before plunging down.

A flash of metallic blue or bright orange, depending on what catches the light, is the best view most of us get of a kingfisher.

**Juveniles** (above) must learn to fish quickly or they will starve. Kingfishers are usually double-brooded, enabling populations to recover quickly after hard winters, when many die.

**Adult.** Short-tailed and dumpy, Kingfishers are perhaps surprisingly small – smaller than a starling. They sit on a small overhanging branch staring intently into the water below.

# GREAT SPOTTED WOODPECKER

## 23 CM, 9 IN

WIDESPREAD IN BRITISH WOODLANDS BUT ABSENT IN IRELAND. The larger and commoner of the two spotted woodpeckers. Not uncommon in gardens, even feeding on nut bags. Compared with Lesser Spotted, Great is clearly larger and has conspicuous white shoulder patches on either side of a black back (Lesser Spotted is finely barred in this area). The call is a short liquid "tchik", which becomes more varied and bubbly when birds are breeding and displaying. It drums loudly in spring (beginning in February). Both sexes have red undertails. The male has a red nape, distinguishing it clearly from the female, and the juvenile has a red crown (although this disappears in autumn when the bird moults). The flight is undulating, the bird regularly closing its wings and dropping, before flapping again; this style is typical of woodpeckers.

**Female** (above left) and **male in breeding** plumage. Dead and dying trees are a good source of food, the birds extract insects and larvae with their strong bills.

**Juvenile** (left). The stump of a dead birch tree is actually a favourite site to excavate a nest cavity, which may take two weeks to complete. Easy to locate when the young are noisy.

Watch the bird in flight and it is clearly identified by its large white shoulder patches and bright red undertail.

# LESSER SPOTTED WOODPECKER

14.5 CM, 5.75 IN

LESS COMMON THAN GREAT SPOTTED. Found in southern England and Wales, but absent farther north and in Ireland. Lesser Spotted really is tiny – the size of a House Sparrow. Its drumming and singing in early spring often draw attention to its presence. The call is a high-pitched "kikikiki" (not unlike a speeded up Kestrel!). Compared with Great Spotted, Lesser is clearly smaller and has fine barring over the back and closed wings (Great Spotted has large white shoulder patches). The male has a red crown, the female a pale one. The flight is typical undulating woodpecker style, but – because of the birds small size – this often doesn't immediately catch the eye. Look for it high in the tree canopy where it likes to feed. With practice, it is possible to distinguish the longer more high-pitched drumming of Lesser Spotted compared with Great.

Likewise, a practised eye can distinguish between the different sized nest holes of the different woodpecker species. Lessers rarely visit gardens, preferring woods and parkland.

Lesser Spots are distinguished by the fine black and white barring across the back and wings. **Juveniles** (right) have a red crown.

The **male** (below) is recognized by his striking red crown. Both birds excavate the nest cavity which is often on the underside of a dead branch and usually hard to find.

**Female in breeding plumage.** Nest holes are found at every level among the trees, a few feet above ground to over 70 ft high in the branches.

# GREEN WOODPECKER

## 32 CM, 12.5 IN

THE LARGEST BRITISH WOODPECKER. Widespread in wood and parkland, though scarcer in Scotland (but increasing) and absent from Ireland. Frequently seen on the ground – including lawns and dunes – where it hunts for ants, and hops along rather clumsily. Using its strong bill and long tongue it explores the galleries deep in the ant hill, extracting ants and pupae. The olive-green plumage is quite different from the other British woodpeckers. When it flies, it flashes a yellow rump, that has often lead to claims of Golden Oriole (see page 234). Green Woodpeckers drum less often than the other species, but draw attention to themselves by their noisy laughing call (its colloquial name is "yaffle"). Juveniles are heavily streaked and barred on the underparts and have less vivid red heads.

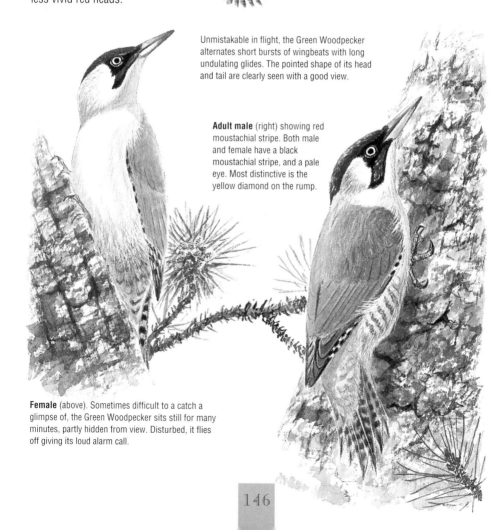

Unmistakable in flight, the Green Woodpecker alternates short bursts of wingbeats with long undulating glides. The pointed shape of its head and tail are clearly seen with a good view.

**Adult male** (right) showing red moustachial stripe. Both male and female have a black moustachial stripe, and a pale eye. Most distinctive is the yellow diamond on the rump.

**Female** (above). Sometimes difficult to a catch a glimpse of, the Green Woodpecker sits still for many minutes, partly hidden from view. Disturbed, it flies off giving its loud alarm call.

# SHORELARK

## 16.5 CM, 6.5 IN

A RARE BIRD, WHICH OCCURS IN SMALL FLOCKS, mainly on the east coast in late autumn and winter. It does indeed feed almost exclusively on shingly shores, or on nearby saltmarshes, but Skylarks also occur in the same habitat, and usually in much larger numbers! Slightly smaller than Skylark, and a shade paler brown and less scaly on the upperparts. The most obvious feature is the face pattern, which – on the male – is yellow, with black on forehead, cheeks and breast. As it attains breeding plumage it develops two small black "horns". This pattern is much fainter in females and young birds, but is always still noticeable and distinctive. In flight, it shows white outer tail feathers, but no white trailing edge. The call is a thin "tsee ree" (thinner than Skylark's buzzy squeak call). Winter flocks tend to be faithful to the same area until they leave in spring. To be honest, it would be unusual – and lucky – to come across Shorelarks that other birdwatchers haven't already found!

A winter flock of Shorelarks characterized by their undulating flight. A scarce bird seen mainly on the east coast where it feeds along the shore line and nearby saltmarshes and dunes.

**Female** (left) and **male in breeding plumage.** The bright yellow of the male is duller in winter. Shorelarks walk and run along the ground in search of food.

# WOODLARK

## 15 CM, 6 IN

A RATHER SCARCE BREEDING BIRD, in very specific type of habitat: not strictly speaking woods. It prefers heath or downland, with scattered trees, and is particularly fond of recently cleared areas, usually near or among conifers. Breeds in southern England and parts of Wales only. These are areas also frequented by Skylarks, so careful identification is required. Woodlark is slightly smaller. The face and head have a much stronger pattern, with a conspicuous pale stripe over the eye, and joining at the back of the neck; more clearly defined cheek, with a rusty interior, and a small – but surprisingly obvious – black and white "notch" at the shoulder of the closed wing. The call is a rather lovely fluty "tit loo eeet"; and the song is sweeter and less frantic than Skylark, often heard at dawn before it is even light. Woodlarks are scarce away from their breeding haunts, but single birds are occasionally seen on passage, usually in October or November .

The wings have no white trailing edge, and the tail has white only at the tips. This gives Woodlark a plainer overall look than Skylark when it flies.

**Adult in spring plumage**. On the ground, Woodlark gives a clear view of the characteristic black and white wing "notch", and the pale stripe over the eye.

# SKYLARK

## 18 CM, 7 IN

WIDESPREAD BREEDING BIRD, FOUND IN MORE OR LESS ALL TREELESS HABITATS, except the very tops of mountains. Most easily identified by its effusive song, delivered from way up in the sky, before it closes its wings, drops into cover and then walks to its nest (i.e. it doesn't drop *onto* the nest.) Skylarks are also migrants and considerable movements, especially in late autumn, involve both British birds and continental immigrants. Individual migrants are the birds most likely to cause identification puzzles, as they are similar to other lark species and pipits. Skylark is rather bulky, and tends to shuffle along, crouched rather low to the ground when feeding. It has conspicuous white outer tail feathers, but this is a feature shown by several other streaky little brown birds: for example, pipits and female buntings. Skylark's call is also distinctive: a slightly bubbly "prrp prrp". Birds in winter sometimes make a odd short squeaky call, which can be puzzling at first. For detailed differences with Shorelark and Woodlark (see pages 147 and 148). A good general point is that Skylark has the plainest face.

Skylark shows its most unique feature when it flies; a white trailing edge to its wings found in no other British lark. Its song flight can last up to five minutes.

**Winter.** When they are not singing, Skylarks spend their time on the ground. They sometimes form quite large flocks in winter, usually on stubble or freshly disturbed fields.

**Summer plumage.** When disturbed, Skylark tends to crouch rather than run. Crest not always obvious. It is usually seen when a bird is excited or alarmed.

# SWIFT
## 16.5 CM, 6.5 IN

OFTEN SEEN FLYING WITH SWALLOWS AND MARTINS (pages 151–153). Swifts are summer visitors, one of the latest to arrive – usually in very late April, more commonly in May – and one of the earliest to leave, being rarely seen in numbers after early August. Compared with swallows and martins, Swifts are larger, with narrow crescent-shaped wings, and forked tail, often held closed. A flying sickle! The plumage looks all black, though there is a small pale patch on the throat, more conspicuous in young birds. The call also draws attention: a high-pitched "screaming", particularly noisy when birds first arrive and chase around in parties displaying. Their diet consists wholly of insects caught on the wing, in abundance in warm summer weather. Swifts are seen feeding over built-up areas, open country and fresh water. Swifts never perch on wires and are usually only seen to land as they disappear into their nests under the eaves.

A really remarkable bird, the Swift spends most of its life flying. Watch them spiralling up into the sky on a calm evening to sleep on the wing.

**Adults.** Swift roosts only when nesting and may fly more than 1 million miles in its lifetime. Juveniles leave the nest, flying south without their parents and may remain on the wing for two years.

# SAND MARTIN
## 12 CM, 4.75 IN

THE SMALLEST AND "FEEBLEST" OF THE HIRUNDINES (SWALLOW FAMILY), with rather weak, fluttery flight. The upperparts are sandy brown and the underparts white but with a narrow brown breast band. In flight it lacks the darkness of either Swallow or House Martin and has no white rump or tail streamers. Sand Martins are one of the first migrants to arrive, often in early March in southern counties, but they rarely linger long into September. Migrants at both ends of the season often gather over lakes and reservoirs, where they mix with other hirundines in their search for insects. They nest in burrows in "traditional" colonies in river banks, sea cliffs or quarries. Sand Martins excavate burrows at least 1 m (3 ft) deep and may remove stones several times their own weight. A few years ago numbers dropped considerably, probably due to droughts in Africa, but recent years have seen a recovery. Found all over Britain, and particularly numerous along Scottish rivers. Call is a dry "tchrrup", clearly different from House Martin, also incorporated into its chattery song.

On the wing, Sand Martin is easily distinguished from other hirundines by its shorter and only slightly forked tail. Its call is harsher than the Swallow or House Martin's.

Sand Martins are gregarious birds, nesting in colonies and clinging to the banks containing their nests. Outside the breeding season, before migrating they roost socially, particularly in reedbeds.

Upperparts sandy-brown, underparts white with narrow brown breast band. The smallest of the swallow family.

# SWALLOW

SWALLOW AND MARTINS BELONG TO A FAMILY CALLED HIRUNDINES (hirondelle is the French for swallow). There are three common British species (see House and Sand Martin, pages 153 and 151). All are summer visitors. Swallows differ from martins in having longer wings and tail streamers, and a red throat above a bluish breast band. At rest, they are easily identified. In flight, Swallow looks more streamlined and shows an all dark head. Swift is larger, with crescent-shaped wings, and looks completely black (see page 150). Young birds have short streamers and the red on the face is a more washed out dull pink. Swallows nest is an open mud cup, usually on a beam of a barn or outhouse, and they will often return to the same site year after year. Large numbers roost in reedbeds in the autumn before migrating. The call is a twittery "tswit", and the song an excitable longer version, with a similarly twittery character.

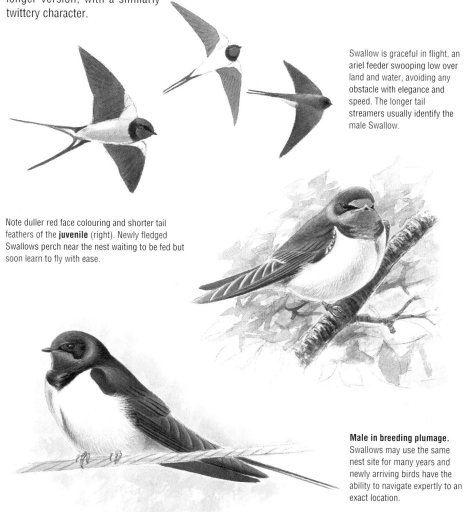

Swallow is graceful in flight, an ariel feeder swooping low over land and water, avoiding any obstacle with elegance and speed. The longer tail streamers usually identify the male Swallow.

Note duller red face colouring and shorter tail feathers of the **juvenile** (right). Newly fledged Swallows perch near the nest waiting to be fed but soon learn to fly with ease.

**Male in breeding plumage.** Swallows may use the same nest site for many years and newly arriving birds have the ability to navigate expertly to an exact location.

# HOUSE MARTIN
## 12.5 CM, 5 IN

A SUMMER VISITOR, USUALLY ARRIVING A FEW DAYS LATER THAN SWALLOW and often lingering later in the autumn. Most easily separated from Swallow in flight, by its pure white rump. Otherwise, the upperparts are velvety black (compared with bluish-black in Swallow and sandy-brown Sand Martin) and the underparts pure white. An unusual feature, sometimes seen when House Martin is perched or clinging by the nest, are the short legs and feet which have tiny white feathers even on the toes. The flight style is just a little less graceful than Swallow, with broader based wings, and they often fly higher when hunting insects. The tail is forked, but with no streamers. House Martins build mud ball nests under the guttering of buildings, often in large colonies. Before there were buildings they presumably nested on cliffs. However, sadly and mysteriously, many of these colonies appear to be dwindling in recent years. The call is a cheerful "chirrupping", also incorporated into the more twittery song. Found all over Britain, but scarcer in the far north.

Both male and female birds work at nest-building. The entrance is small and always at the top under the eaves. Very occasionally House Martins build inside roof spaces or outbuildings.

House Martin spends much time on the wing but also perches readily on telegraph wires and buildings. **Juvenile** (right), **adult birds** (far right) feed their browner coloured fledglings both at the nest and in flight.

The pure white rump of House Martin is unmistakable. Less dramatic in flight than Swallow, this sociable bird has a softer and sweeter song, heard through the summer months.

14 CM, 6 IN

PIPITS ARE SMALL STREAKY BROWN BIRDS, with fine thin beaks, which spend most of their time on the ground, usually in short grass. All British species have white (or whitish) outer tail feathers and in this respect, they are similar to larks. Meadow Pipit is by far the most numerous and widespread. It is by no means confined to meadows. It may well be the only small breeding bird on remote moorland, and in winter it often occurs in all kinds of habitats, from sewage farms to saltmarshes, and even on urban wasteland. Meadow Pipit migration is in fact very complex, with some British birds going south in winter and north in spring, and other continental birds arriving in autumn. There are some days at coastal locations when the headlands seem to be alive with Meadow Pipits. They also travel inland routes. Tree Pipit is very similar in plumage, but is only a summer visitor, though it may occur in similar (treeless) areas on passage. By far the best distinction is call, and fortunately, pipits invariably call when they fly.

In the breeding season, Meadow Pipit displays with an attractive song-flight, rising with a wispy crescendo and then parachuting down with a series of sweeter notes ending in a trill.

Out of the breeding season, its call is a thin "tseep", a clear sound that will often attract the attention of migrating birds overhead.

Pipits are similar to larks, but have more slender beaks and are generally slimmer and more slender-winged.

# TREE PIPIT

## 15 CM, 6 IN

A SUMMER VISITOR. SO, ANY WINTER PIPIT WON'T BE A TREE! Breeds in open heathy type woodlands, often in the same sort of habitat as Woodlarks. Requires a few large trees, where it can perch right on the top, often delivering part of its song. The full song, however, is usually given in flight. It is often this that draws attention to the bird's presence. Away from the breeding areas, Tree Pipits occur as passage migrants, often in company with Meadow Pipits, and frequently in treeless areas. The call is a distinctive hoarse "teeze". The plumage is very similar to Meadow Pipit, though there are some rather subtle differences, such as slightly pinker legs, a faint yellowy wash on the breast, and a more obvious bar (greater coverts) on the closed wing. If it takes cover in a tree, it tends to creep along the branch gently wagging its tail. Note, however, that Meadow Pipits *do* sometimes perch in trees. Does not occur in flocks like Meadow Pipits.

Like most pipits, Tree is a ground-feeding and nesting bird but quickly flies to seek cover in a tree if disturbed.

**Male** Tree Pipit (above) rises from its perch and begins singing near the peak of ascent, continuing with a descending "twsee wee wee" as it parachutes down, wings and tail spread, to land on the same perch.

Best distinguished from Meadow Pipit by its call and song flight. It also happens to have a shorter hind claw, but you won't see that!

# ROCK PIPIT

## 17 CM, 6.5 IN

NOT A BAD NAME, AS ROCK PIPITS DO VERY MUCH PREFER ROCKY COASTLINES, although they also occasionally crop up on inland reservoirs (but usually concrete ones). But Meadow Pipits also occur in the same areas. A little larger than Meadow Pipit, and darker and greyer, with noticeably darker legs, often with a dark red tinge (Meadow Pipits tend to be pinky or yellowy). The outer tail feathers are smoky grey, not white. Well camouflaged among the rocks, this bird is often unseen until it takes to the wing. The call is often written as "fist", and is similar to Meadow Pipit, but distinguishable with experience. Found all round Britain, but scarce in south-east England. Never forms flocks as large as Meadow Pipit: you rarely see more than a dozen or so together, even in winter. Nests in crevices and is known to be a host species for cuckoos. It has a typical pipit song flight, rising up from a rock on the shoreline and singing as it descends, ending with the characteristic trill.

Rock Pipit's flight-song is similar to Meadow's but louder and stronger and perhaps rather more musical. Its call is fuller and more metallic.

**Adults.** Rock Pipit is a resident bird, usually staying within its chosen territory and may be seen searching out insects and small molluscs among the rocks and seaweed of the shoreline.

# WATER PIPIT

### 17 CM, 6.5 IN

ONCE CONSIDERED THE SAME SPECIES AS ROCK PIPIT, but is clearly different and now accepted as such! A winter visitor only, to certain favoured sites, mainly sewage farms, cress beds, freshwater marshes or river foreshores. Around one hundred Water Pipits are recorded in Britain each year, most frequently in the south and east of England. The earliest sightings are usually in October and by April most have returned to their breeding grounds high in the mountains of central and southern Europe. Much the same build as Rock Pipit, but brown rather than greyish upperparts, and with a whitish stripe above the eye, and white (not grey) outer tail feathers. The call is "fist", similar to Rock Pipit. The streaking on the underparts reduces as winter goes on, and by spring some birds attain breeding plumage. This is very attractive, with a bluey grey back and almost unstreaked underparts, flushed with pink. I once saw a migrant like this on a dry coastal headland: at a distance, it looked rather like a male Wheatear! (see page 167).

Pure white outer tail feathers and a pale stripe over the eye are hallmarks of Water Pipit. Very similar to Meadow Pipit in song.

Adults in the attractive pale colours of **breeding plumage** (above) and the darker **shades of winter** (right). This rare winter visitor has dark legs similar to the Rock Pipit. At the best of times Water Pipit is difficult to observe. It tends to fly off as soon as seen and move a long distance before alighting again.

# YELLOW WAGTAIL
## 16.5 CM, 6.5 IN

A SUMMER VISITOR. So any wagtail with yellow on it during winter months will be a Grey. Yellow Wagtail breeds in damp meadows and marshes, more usually (but not exclusively) near the sea, or large inland waters. Mainly in central and south-eastern England. It also occurs on passage, but is a scarce bird in Scotland and particularly in Ireland. Male is bright yellow below and olive above (unlike the grey of Grey Wagtail). Female and young birds are much duller, and some can be quite brown and washed out, but there is always a tinge of yellow. Juveniles often have a few dark flecks across the upper breast, and can slightly resemble a large pipit (particularly the rare Tawny Pipit). The call is a loud "fsweep", which may draw attention to birds flying over. Several races of Yellow Wagtail occur in Britain on migration (and may very occasionally breed), but none are anything like as common as the basic all-yellow form. The most frequent is Blue-headed Wagtail, which does indeed have a pale blue head.

Many different races of Yellow Wagtail have been identified. Several occur in Britain on passage – the one you are most likely to see is the **Blue-headed** (right).

Yellow rump, no wingbar. Yellow Wagtail has bounding song flight.

**Juveniles** (right) are pale, sometimes quite washed out, with a few dark flecks forming a band across the upper breast.

**Male** (right) is olive, with yellow underparts; **female** (above) paler. Although the males of the various races can usually be identified by head pattern, it's just about impossible with females and young birds.

### 18 CM, 7 IN

GREY ABOVE BUT LEMON YELLOW BELOW, with the colour particularly strong under the tail. The male has a black bib. Breeds near fast-flowing streams, mainly in upland areas but sometimes near – or even in – towns or villages. Your best chance of seeing them is usually to stand on a bridge and scan along the river banks. The birds teeter among pebbles and on stones. In winter, they move to lower locations, which may include urban lakes or canals and nearby rooftops. The call is shorter than Pied Wagtail, with more of a "zing" to it : a sharp "tzit". It may share its habitat with Pied Wagtail; but would very rarely be seen alongside Yellow Wagtail, so confusion shouldn't occur. If you can see the leg colour, Grey Wagtail's are pink and Yellow's are black! In flight, Grey has a longer tail, that looks exceptionally narrow at the base and this can be noticeable even at a considerable distance.

Grey sports the longest tail of all its family, narrow and black with white outer feathers. A delight to watch, perched on a boulder as this **female** is, or flying out over the water chasing insects.

**Male in summer plumage** with the distinctive black throat. Grey is usually solitary but a few may be seen feeding together along stretches of water where insects are plentiful.

# PIED WAGTAIL

## 18 CM, 7 IN

THERE ARE THREE COMMON SPECIES OF BRITISH WAGTAIL. All well named, in that they do indeed have long tails which they wag. Otherwise, they all look very different and have differing habitat preferences. Pied Wagtail is the most numerous and widespread. Breeds all over Britain, often – but not always – near water, and forms large roosting flocks in winter, often gathering in very urban areas, such as factories or car parks. Pied Wagtail nests often play host to the Cuckoo. Both male and female are pied (black and white) though the female has a greyer back and smaller black bib. Young birds have a messier and slightly brown-tinged plumage. The call is best remembered as "chiswick" (as in the London Borough of). The continental race – known as White Wagtail – occurs on passage in small numbers, particularly in spring.

The flight is bounding (undulating), and the birds often call as they fly. Often seen near or amongst buildings and may even nest there.

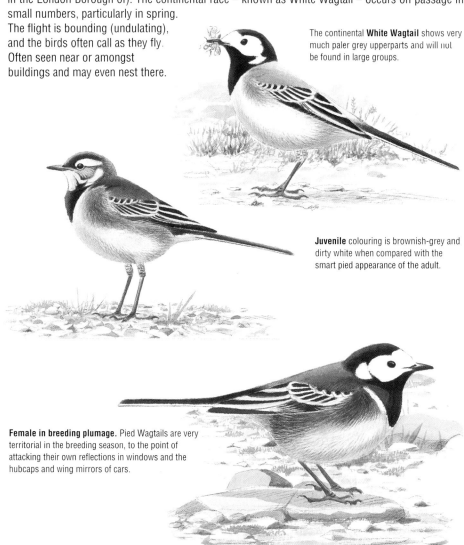

The continental **White Wagtail** shows very much paler grey upperparts and will not be found in large groups.

**Juvenile** colouring is brownish-grey and dirty white when compared with the smart pied appearance of the adult.

**Female in breeding plumage.** Pied Wagtails are very territorial in the breeding season, to the point of attacking their own reflections in windows and the hubcaps and wing mirrors of cars.

# WAXWING

18 CM, 7 IN

A WINTER VISITOR FROM THE FAR NORTH OF EUROPE AND RUSSIA, which sometimes invades Britain in large numbers, while in other years there are almost none. These irruptions depend on food supply (or rather, lack of it). Waxwings are completely addicted to red berries, so if there is a Waxwing winter, look for them on any red berry bearing bushes and trees. The largest flocks often occur alongside supermarkets or petrol stations, where the borders have been "decoratively" planted. Waxwings are normally very tame, and will allow close approach, in busy areas. They may also visit gardens. They arrive – usually in October or November – mainly on the east and north-east coasts, but then move inland, sometimes reaching Ireland. They are slightly smaller than a Starling, but the pinkish-brown plumage, crest and waxy red and yellow tipped wings are unique. A flock in flight, however, could easily be dismissed as Starlings, as they have a similar shape. The call is a soft sibilant trilling.

An irruption of waxwings is a winter bonus to the birdwatcher. These are not shy birds and a small flock may stay around one berry-laden bush for several days.

**Male** (below), a striking bird with prominent crest and red and yellow wing and tail markings. **Female** (left). The sexes are not always easy to distinguish although the female colouring is often less intense.

161

# DIPPER

18 CM, 7 IN

A SMALL PLUMP BIRD, WITH THE LOOKS OF A THRUSH AND THE HABITS OF A SUBMARINE! Found exclusively near fast-flowing streams, mainly in upland areas, though may descend lower during the winter, but always near water. If seen well, it is unmistakable, looking mainly black above, with a chestnut belly and a gleaming white bib. Your best chance of a good view is to wait at a bridge and scan the rocks and riverbanks, where the birds bob up and down, before leaping into the water, often submerging in their quest for food. Grey Wagtails often share this habitat. Dippers bob and curtsey with a downward jerk of the tail and a blink of their eyes. If close enough you may see the white eye-lid. Young Dippers are greyer and scalier. Once seen, never forgotten, but Dippers also have a habit of disappearing round the next corner without giving a decent view! The flight is very fast, low and direct. The call is a short "zit", and the song a pleasantly sweet warble.

Slate-grey plumage of **juvenile**. Dippers are usually solitary or in pairs, preferring the same stretch of water all year. Bridges, overhanging banks, tree roots and waterfalls all provide nest sites.

**Adult plumage.** Among songbirds the elusive Dipper is unique, diving into the water and walking or flying along the bottom searching for food. A strong swimmer without webbed feet!

# WREN
## 9.5 CM, 3.75 IN

ARGUABLY BRITAIN'S COMMONEST AND MOST WIDESPREAD BIRD, but not perhaps obviously so, since it is small and often secretive. Wrens breed all over Britain and may be found nesting among rocks on remote islands, as well as in dense undergrowth in the corner of an urban garden. The nest is a lovely compact ball of dead leaves and moss. The bird itself is pretty unmistakable: tiny, plump and with an invariably cocked tail. It also has an extremely loud song, always incorporating a fast trill, and often delivered from a conspicuous perch, with a puffed out breast and trembling wings. The call is a hard "tchick tchick", and is sometimes the only hint of the bird's presence when it is in skulking mode. This habit of giving only brief glimpses has led many a birdwatcher to momentarily mistake Wrens for skulky rare warblers.

The nest is often stuffed into the tiniest crevice. Males may build several nests for the female to choose from. The female adds the lining! Males may be polygamous.

Wrens often sing from conspicuous perches, but even if you can't see it, it makes its presence felt. Always a good rule if you are in pursuit of a possible skulky rarity: ask yourself are you sure it isn't just a wayward Wren?

Fast and direct flight, on whirring wings, though usually only short distances.

# DUNNOCK

### 14.5 CM, 5.75 IN

SOMETIMES ALSO CALLED HEDGE SPARROW, but it is not a true sparrow. (Sparrows are seed-eaters with stubby bills). Actually belongs to the Accentor family (yet another name is Hedge Accentor), which are small fairly secretive birds with thin beaks. Dunnocks are found all over Britain, and – though they prefer foliage – they also occur in quite remote and bleak habitats. Both male and female are dingy brown on the upperparts with strong streaking, and grey head and breast, with a slightly bluish tinge. Although this is a rather featureless plumage, there is really nothing else like it. Female House Sparrow is most similar, but is instantly identified by its stubby beak. Dunnocks typically feed on the ground, in the shade, and they hop with little shuffly movements. They frequently flick their wings. The call is a loud "tseep", and the song an attractive wispy but quite busy warble. A bit like a Wren's call, but without the power or the trill.

**Young birds** are a little spottier than the adults, which perhaps most often are confused with female House Sparrows, but Dunnocks are much greyer and have a fine beak.

Its skulking behaviour can lead birdwatchers a dance if they feel they have had a glimpse of a rare warbler. Many a possible rarity turns out to be a Dunnock!

Wing flicking is characteristic Dunnock behaviour (yet another traditional name is Shufflewing). Usually feeds on the ground and rarely feeds on a birdtable.

# ROBIN
## 14 CM, 5.5 IN

POSSIBLY THE BEST LOVED AND BEST KNOWN BIRD IN BRITAIN. The adult hardly needs a description. Juveniles, however, can be puzzling, as they are speckled all over. British Robins are very tame and conspicuous, but Continental birds are very skulky, and when they occur here on migration (which they do in considerable numbers) they are likely to keep hidden or give only brief glimpses. This behaviour has led many a birdwatcher to mistake a briefly seen Robin for any number of possible rare little brown birds. They can skulk like warblers or flit like flycatchers. So, if you are wondering if you are chasing a rarity, it is never a bad rule to ask yourself if it might just be a shy Robin! Fortunately, the Robin's most frequent call is very distinctive: a loud "tick tick". The song is full of lovely relaxed wispy phrases, the winter version is audibly "sadder". Robins often sing at night, and are mistaken for Nightingales (see page 166).

**Juveniles** are speckled with buffy spots and do not have a red breast. The colour soon develops, but is patchy at first, and the birds look even odder for a week or so.

Highly territorial, the Robin's aggression is triggered by the red breast of another. Males and females hold separate territories during the winter.

16.5 CM, 6.5 IN

NIGHTINGALES ARE SUMMER VISITORS, and occur in only relatively few areas of south-eastern England. So, if you hear a bird singing at night, at any time except spring and early summer, or away from the south and east, it is *not* a Nightingale! The confusions arise because, in fact, several species do often sing at night: particularly Robin, Song Thrush and Blackbird. Nightingales like open woodland with dense thickets, often near heathland. They don't occur in town (so the bird that sang in Berkeley Square wasn't one!). Nightingale's song is indeed very rich and fruity, incorporating various trills and drawn out whistles, and is delivered just as much during the day as at night. Nightingales are a little bigger and more slender than a Robin, warm brown above, paler below, and with a distinct rufous tinge to the tail. Not dissimilar to a female Redstart but Redstarts are smaller, and the red tail contrasts more with the rest of the plumage, and it is "trembled" frequently (see Redstart, page 169).

**Juveniles** are spotted and look rather like a big young Robin.

Nightingales are real skulkers, and you rarely get a good view of one. When you do, you realize it isn't much to look at! **Adult plumage** might be confused with female Redstart (which may well occur in similar habitat). Warm brown above, pale below.

# WHEATEAR

## 14.5–15 CM, 5.75–6 IN

A SUMMER VISITOR, and in fact often the first migrant to arrive in spring (early March). Larger and slimmer than Robin. Prefers open habitats, often with few or no trees. Breeds on uplands, but occurs on migration both inland and at the coast, often on playing fields or mown turf (for example, around reservoirs). Rather bizarrely, the male shares its lovely colour scheme with the entirely woodland loving Nuthatch (page 197), and I have heard of them being confused by a beginner looking at pictures in the book, but not reading the text! Wheatears don't creep up tree trunks! Wheatears do perch on bushes and walls, and even sometimes on the top of isolated trees and, at a distance, their "jizz" is not dissimilar to Whinchat. Note the lack of Whinchat's white eyestripe, and note the white rump as soon as it flies. The call is a hard "chack chack", and it has a rather squeaky wheezy song, often delivered in flight. They also sometimes hover like tiny Kestrels in search of food.

Females, juveniles and non breeding males lack the mask and can be duller grey or brown on the upperparts.

As soon as it flies, it shows a bright white rump, which is unique to the species (the name means "white arse" in old Norse!).

Juvenile. Spends most of its time on the ground, where it runs in fits and starts and then pauses in rather upright pose.

Female (above). The male (right) has a grey back, black wings and mask, and can be quite peachy colour underneath. At a distance, the pale breast stands out.

# BLACK REDSTART

## 14 CM, 5.5 IN

THE SAME SIZE AND JIZZ AS A REDSTART, but the male is very dark grey, and actually black on the face and breast, with white flashes in the wing, whilst the female is merely dingy all over. Both have the typical quivering orangey tail. Black Redstarts, however, do not occur in woods. They prefer rocks, or even concrete, and, in fact, their favourite breeding places are ruined buildings, power stations and factories, mainly in central and south-eastern England. At such places, they sing from rooftop perches. The song is an accelerating warble (a little like a Chaffinch) ending in a rattly trill. The call is a hard "tuck". Black Redstarts stay in Britain in winter, and usually move down to the coasts, where they may frequent shingly beaches or rocky shorelines. There is also a noticeable passage, especially in October, when they often favour newly ploughed fields (as do other migrants, such as Wheatears). So, any Redstart in winter will be a Black. However, Black Redstart is never as numerous a migrant as Common Redstart can be.

**Females** are always sootier than female Redstart but some individuals are quite hard to judge! Juveniles are spotted, rather like young Robins. Bright red tail gives the bird its name.

**Male in breeding plumage.** Black on the throat and with white wing flashes, and, of course, the red tail, which is constantly shimmered.

**Male in non breeding plumage** is greyer. Any Redstart in winter will be a Black one. Not a common breeding species, but in autumn quite a number fly through on passage.

# REDSTART
### 14 CM, 5.5 IN

A SUMMER VISITOR, QUITE WIDELY DISTRIBUTED IN BRITAIN but by no means common. Breeds in woods, parkland and the edges of heath or moorland, but requires mature trees with nesting holes. About the size of a Robin, but slimmer and with the tail invariably held down. The male in breeding plumage is very striking with a black bib, deep orange-red breast and orange rump and tail. Female is much duller: generally fawn, with only the tail orange. Young males can show partial breeding plumage. Redstarts habitually quiver or tremble their tails. The call is a loud "hoo eet". (Unfortunately, several other species also give "hooeet" calls: for example, Chaffinch, Willow Warbler and Chiffchaff). This call is often incorporated into the jangling little song. Redstarts also occur on migration at coastal sites, which may be completely treeless. At such times and places, Black Redstarts may also occur. Both male and female Black Redstart are uniformly dark, except for the tail, but the palest females are only a few shades duskier than female Redstart.

**Male in breeding plumage** (below). Starts to look more like female (though still darker) by autumn migration.

**Female** (right). Nests in mature trees such as oak, with suitable holes, though it will occasionally also use walls or nest on the ground.

**Young male** with just a hint of the black throat coming into view.

# WHINCHAT

## 12.5 CM, 5 IN

SLIGHTLY SMALLER AND SLIMMER THAN A ROBIN. A summer visitor, breeding in open heathland and young conifer plantations, especially in the north and west of Britain. Also turns up on migration, sometimes in less rural areas, such as playing fields and allotments. Whinchats make themselves conspicuous by perching on top of bushes, dead plants, fences and even on telegraph wires. Most similar in plumage and habits to Stonechat, but Stonechats are dumpier and lack the obvious white eyebrow stripe, and "capped" appearance of Whinchat. Whinchat also has white sides to the base of the tail, most noticeable in males when they fly or land. At a distance, Whinchat can be mistaken for Wheatear, which is a similar shape, and also often perches in similar habitats. But note Wheatear's vivid white rump as soon as it flies. Males are brighter than females and juveniles, with blacker ears and upperparts. Song is similar to Stonechat's and call is "tic-tic" but it is almost always silent away from the breeding areas.

**Females and juveniles** are much more likely to be confused with Stonechats, but note that the eyestripe is still conspicuous.

In flight shows white sides to the base of tail. Compare with Stonechat.

**Male** has obvious creamy white eyestripe. Upright stance, with bobbing and flicking of tail and wings. Often active into late evening, up to darkness setting in.

# STONECHAT

## 12.5 CM, 5 IN

A DUMPY LITTLE BIRD – SLIGHTLY SMALLER THAN A ROBIN, but rather similar shape – that makes itself conspicuous by perching on bushes, dead plants, fences and telegraph wires. Breeds on moors and heathland, especially where there is gorse. In winter, moves to lower areas, including waste ground and saltmarshes. Numbers are swelled by continental migrants in late autumn. Most easily confused with Whinchat, which has similar habits. Look at the head: Stonechat does not have a whitish eyestripe, and in flight it lacks the Whinchat's white sides to the tail. Male has obvious black head, with white half collar, and orange breast; but females and juveniles are much duller and spottier. They could be confused with young speckly Robins (page 165) or moulty Redstarts (page 169), but neither are likely to perch out in the open so much. Moulting Stonechats can look particularly scruffy and odd, and have been known to puzzle birdwatchers! The call is a sharp "tsak tsak" (like clinking pebbles), which may attract your attention to the bird.

In flight shows white patch on wing, but not the white sides to tail like Whinchat.

**Female.** Similar jizz and habits to Whinchat but lacks the white eyebrow.

**Juvenile.** Spotty – or is it "messy"?

**Male in fresh breeding plumage.** Gorse is a favourite bush to perch upon and proclaim territory.

# FIELDFARE

## 25.5 CM, 10 IN

THE LARGER OF THE WINTER THRUSHES. Arrives with Scandinavian Redwings in October and is usually gone by the end of April. A very few breed each year in northern areas. Considerably larger than Redwing – nearly as big as a Mistle Thrush – but with very distinctive and handsome plumage. Its speckly breast is on a background of yellowy buff, and no other thrush has its chestnut-brown upperparts and grey head and rump. The grey rump is particularly obvious when birds are in flight, as is the silvery leading edge to the underwing. Fieldfares are noisy birds in flight, usually making loud excitable chacking and wheezing noises. They do travel and call at night along with Redwings, but not quite in such numbers. They feed on berries in hedgerows and in nearby fields. They are almost always in flocks: indeed, it's true to say that if you see a couple of Fieldfares in a tree, there's probably a dozen. When they fly, you will often be surprised how many were in there.

In flight shows silvery grey leading edge to white underwing, but when the bird takes off, the grey rump is probably what will catch your eye.

In hard weather fieldfares may come to gardens to feed. One bird may hog the birdtable, defending it against all comers.

Check hawthorn hedges in autumn and winter for winter thrushes, which will also feed in grassy fields. They will often also visit orchards to clear up any fallen apples or pears.

# REDWING

## 21 CM, 8.25 IN.

THERE ARE TWO SPECIES OF "WINTER THRUSHES" IN BRITAIN: Redwing and Fieldfare. Both arrive in October – often in their thousands – and depart by April. A very few pairs of Redwings breed each year in Scotland, or the Northern Isles. They migrate at night, and their thin squeaky calls are often mistaken for bats (generally people can't actually hear bats!) Redwing is about the size of a Song Thrush, and not dissimilar in plumage, but easily identified by the vivid white stripe over the eye, and white moustache. The red part of the wing is in the "armpit", and is clearly a deeper orange than a Song Thrush. A small red area is usually visible on the flanks of a feeding bird. Redwings are often in flocks with other thrushes, especially Fieldfares. They feed on berries – particularly hawthorns – and on worms, in areas of short grass. Part of our wintering population comes from Greenland and Iceland, and the rest from Scandinavia.

Note red "armpit". Redwings often travel in flocks with other species of thrush, especially Fieldfares.

The edges of playing fields are a good place to look for Redwings in winter. They also feed on fruits and berries.

Smaller than a Fieldfare, about the size of a Song Thrush. Note warm brown colouring and bright eyebrow stripe.

# SONG THRUSH.

## 23 CM, 9 IN

A RESIDENT BREEDING BIRD ALL OVER BRITAIN wherever there are bushes or trees, and numbers are also swelled by continental immigrants in winter. Song and Mistle Thrush are the two resident thrush species, and the most frequently confused. Song is smaller, rather less densely speckled on the underparts, with smaller spots, and lacks the rather patchy face pattern of Mistle Thrush (see Mistle Thrush, opposite, for other differences). In flight, Mistle Thrush shows white outer tail tips, and a whitish underwing (as opposed to the cinnamon of Song Thrush). Song Thrush's song is similar to a Blackbird's, but it repeats each phrase, sometimes several times. It sometimes sings at night, and gets wrongly reported as a Nightingale. In flight, it often gives a short "tsip" call. Sadly, Song Thrushes seem to be declining as garden and farmland birds, possibly as a result of ultra efficient snail control by pesticides. They break snails on a stone "anvil", which is left surrounded by bits of shell.

Flight is reasonably direct. Note pale orange underwing. Not so gregarious as other thrushes.

Although declining, Song Thrushes are still the most familiar "speckled" thrush. Get to know them well and use them as a comparison for the others.

Has a rich and varied song repertoire, but easily told from Blackbird's because each phrase is uttered at least twice. May also sing at night.

# MISTLE THRUSH

### 27 CM, 10.5 IN

THE MISTLE THRUSH IS OUR LARGEST THRUSH, with bold conspicuous breast spots and grey back. Generally, it has less warm coloration than the Song Thrush. It shows white outertail feathers and white underwing in flight, which is characterized by the wings being closed at regular intervals, but not markedly undulating. Fieldfare has similar flight pattern and also has white underwing but upperparts are completely different. The Mistle Thrush is also called Stormcock because of its habit of singing loudly from exposed perches in bad weather. Its song is not repetitive like the Song Thrush's nor so mellow as the Blackbird's. Call is a harsh churr or rattle. Quite shy during breeding season but will defend its territory fiercely against other bird species and even prey on the nestlings of small birds, although most of the time it relies on fruit, berries (including mistletoe of course), insects and other invertebrates. In late summer family parties often move out into more open ground. Present throughout the year, with winter migrants visiting from the continent.

Singing loudly, if not so musically as a Blackbird or Song Thrush, from the top of an exposed perch is typical.

In flight, the white underwing soon separates Mistle from other thrushes except Fieldfare. For that, a back view is easier.

Upright stance, bold attitude and "bouncy" gait. Mistle Thrushes do eat small snails, but a thrush bashing a snail on a stone is almost certainly a Song Thrush!

# BLACKBIRD

## 25 CM, 10 IN

ONE OF BRITAIN'S BEST LOVED AND MOST FAMILIAR BIRDS. Belongs to the thrush family. Only the male is black. Female and young Blackbirds are brown, and the juveniles can look quite orange-tinged and speckly on the breast, which gives them a more thrush-like look (compare Song and Mistle Thrushes pages 174-175) but they never have the black breast spots or sandy upperparts of true thrushes. Blackbirds are found all over Britain, even in fairly wild and almost treeless terrain, but they are missing from the really mountainous areas. Numbers are much increased in winter by continental immigrants. The song is very rich, and sometimes heard at night, giving rise to reports of Nightingales (see page 166). The "chink chink" alarm call is also a familiar sound, and it also has a thin anxiety call "seeee". Ring Ouzel is the most similar species. Particularly beware semi-albino Blackbirds that may have white on their breasts. Ring Ouzel's breast crescent is always more symmetrical (even in the duller females).

**Juvenile** (left) is speckled and rusty-brown. Can look very thrush-like.

**Female** (far right) is less warm brown than juvenile. Blackbirds take a wide variety of food – a tell-tale sign is a rhythmic rustling as they turn over leaves in the undergrowth.

**In breeding plumage, male** has a vivid yellow beak! Cocks tail on landing, lowering it slowly and gracefully. A superb songster, it's a noisy bird, persistently "chinking" at dusk.

176

# RING OUZEL

## 24 CM, 9.5 IN

A SUMMER VISITOR, VERY MUCH THE HIGH ALTITUDE VERSION OF THE BLACKBIRD. Similar size. The male is largely black, and the females and young birds browner, though with a greyer caste than female or young Blackbirds. Male has a conspicuous white crescent on the breast, which is fainter in female and young birds. One of the best features is the silvery caste to the wings, which is particularly noticeable when the bird flies. It also frequently gives its characteristic, dry, excitable "tac" call, which is quite unlike a Blackbird's. Ring Ouzels generally prefer to feed on open grassy areas but readily escape into the cover of nearby trees, gorse or brambles. They do not, however, take to thick woodlands, as Blackbirds often do. The song is like a rather wild, simplified version of a Blackbird, which echoes through the valleys and slopes of its wild breeding habitat.

Beware confusion with partial albino Blackbird.

Ring Ouzels are summer visitors to breeding areas and occur on migration in spring and autumn, often with other thrushes.

**Female** (right). Only faint breast band but note scaly underparts and frosty patch on the wing.

**Male in full breeding plumage** (above). First winter male (left).

# GRASSHOPPER WARBLER
## 13 CM, 5 IN
# SEDGE WARBLER
## 13 CM, 5 IN

IT IS HELPFUL TO DIVIDE THE COMMONER WARBLERS by their habitat preferences: waterside species, tree lovers, and scrub and bramble lovers. Often the most useful approach to identifying them is to start by narrowing them down to their most likely group. All are summer visitors only (except Dartford and Cetti's Warbler). **Grasshopper** is a small streaky warbler, that you are far more likely to hear than see – a long high-pitched "reeling", so called because it is not dissimilar to the sound made by an angler's reel. The bird itself spends most of its time secreted deep in thick low vegetation, sometimes – but by no means always – damp. **Sedge Warbler** is a water lover, but tends to prefer the dryer edges, breeding in tangly vegetation alongside lakes, rivers or marshes over most of Britain. Fortunately, it is not a great skulker and it often gives its song from a conspicuous perch, or even during its short parachuting display flight. The song is very similar to Reed Warbler, but is less repetitiously rhythmic.

**Grasshopper Warbler.** Often reels for a minute or more. Best heard at dawn or dusk, or even at night, but the pitch is such that some people can't hear it.

Heavily streaked on the upperparts; conspicuous pale stripe over the eye is a feature not shown by any other common British warbler. **Juveniles** (right) have a streakier pale crown.

**Sedge Warbler.** The streakiest of the "waterside" warblers. Song often incorporates excitable flourishes and even impersonations of other species. More varied than the monotonous regular rhythm of Reed Warbler.

# REED WARBLER

## 12.5 CM, 5 IN

A GOOD NAME, AS IT IS VERY MUCH ADDICTED TO REEDBEDS. It sometimes shares this habitat with Sedge Warblers, but Reed Warblers really do stay in the reeds, at least when they are breeding, for they rarely nest anywhere else. Birds on migration can occur in dryer areas, particularly at the coast, and sometimes puzzle birdwatchers. The truth is, there are a number of rare warblers that are difficult to identify, but they aren't in this book and, frankly, you are unlikely to see them, unless they have already been located by other birders. Basically, Reed is a similar shape and size to Sedge Warbler, but with smooth plain unstreaked upperparts and no obvious eyestripe (there is a very faint one). The song has a similar scratchy quality to Sedge Warbler (hardly a warble!), but it is less imaginative or excitable, repeating each phrase rather monotonously, in regular rhythm. Reed Warblers are scarce in Scotland or the northern isles. Reed Warblers are one of the most common host species of the Cuckoo.

Song is rather scratchy and monotonous, similar to the Sedge Warbler's, but less imaginative or excitable.

Upperparts a uniform warm brown. Reed warblers seldom fly far at their breeding site. They build a cup-shaped nest of woven grasses, which they sling between two or more reedstems.

# LESSER WHITETHROAT
## 13.5 CM, 5.25 IN

OBVIOUSLY RELATED TO WHITETHROAT, but actually quite easy to identify. Lesser has a duller brown back and wings, a darker mask over the cheeks, gleaming white underparts and black legs (Whitethroat's underparts are always slightly buff washed, and the legs are pinky yellow.) As the name implies, Lesser is also a little smaller and less scruffy. The song starts similarly to Whitethroat, but is shorter and often ends with a short "rattle" (though the repeated note is quite melodious). The call is a hard "tac" (similar to Blackcap). Lesser Whitethroats seem to have a definite preference for mature hedgerows and are often seen a little higher from the ground than Whitethroats. Male builds the nest in hedgerow, leaving the female to line it. Tends to be rather more skulking than Whitethroat in its habits. Has white outer tail feathers, as has Whitethroat. Like all warblers, Lesser Whitethroats can also turn up on migration in much less typical and less vegetated habitats.

**Juvenile.** Like other migrants, Lesser Whitethroats will put on weight by eating a lot before undertaking the long flight. Blackberries ripen at just the right time of year.

Flight is very similar to Whitethroat, but Lesser is more skulking in its habits.

**Adult.** The silky white underparts are often the most conspicuous feature as it slips through vegetation.

# WHITETHROAT
## 14 CM, 5.5 IN

THE COMMONEST AND MOST WIDESPREAD OF THE SCRUB-LOVING WARBLERS (known by birdwatchers as Sylvias because this is the first part of their scientific name). They breed in brambles, nettle beds, gorse and similar vegetation. Most conspicuous in the breeding season, when the male gives his scratchy little song, either from a perch or during his parachuting display flight. At other times, Whitethroats can be very skulky. The male has the greyer head and the more obvious white throat, which is sometimes fluffed out, giving the bird a slightly scruffy look. Females and juveniles are duller, though the young birds do have a rather nice tawny tinge to the upperparts. Lesser Whitethroat may share not dissimilar habitats, but is duller brown on the back, has a dark mask and black legs. Whitethroats have pinky yellow legs (see Lesser Whitethroat, opposite). The most frequently heard call is a soft scolding "churr". Has white outer tail feathers, as has Lesser Whitethroat. Although, like other warblers, largely insectivorous, berries are an important part of its food in the autumn.

Often flashes its white outer tail feathers as it flicks into cover. Whitethroat has scratchy little song which may be given from a perch or in parachute display flight.

**Male** (far right). Mask is not so dark as in Lesser Whitethroat.

**Female.** Whitethroats nest in brambles and low bushes, building a rather larger nest than Lesser Whitethroat's.

**Juvenile** is very like female but smarter and cleaner – because it's younger! Usually two broods are reared.

# GARDEN WARBLER

## 14 CM, 5.5 IN

NOT REALLY A VERY APPROPRIATE NAME, as this species isn't often seen in gardens, unless they have been left to get thoroughly overgrown. Garden Warblers prefer the tangly, brambly edges to woodlands. They are scrub lovers, but seem to need mature trees nearby. They are clearly related to Blackcap, and – like that species – are rather slow and cumbersome movers through foliage: lumbering, rather than flitting like the more agile warblers. Most of the time it stays under cover. The plumage is very plain: a soft greyish brown, with no obvious markings, though there might be a very slight olive tinge on the neck. Garden Warbler is rather like a Blackcap without a cap! The song is very similar indeed to the Blackcap's, and often confuses even experienced ears. It contains much the same notes but is a little more compressed and less rambly, but individuals vary.

Perhaps the most likely confusion species would be a dull Chiffchaff (see Chiffchaff) but note Garden Warbler's larger size and less agile movements.

Rarely seen out in the open, the **adult** Garden Warbler stays under thick cover most of the time. It likes broadleaf or mixed woodland with dense, brambly undergrowth for nesting.

**Juveniles** (above) are very like the adults. A single brood is generally reared and young birds remain with the female for several weeks after leaving the nest.

# BLACKCAP

## 14 CM, 5.5 IN

SMALL SIZE AND JIZZ TO GARDEN WARBLER, that is larger and slower than most warblers. Plumage is a rather leaden greyish. The male has a black cap, the female and youngsters have chestnut-brown caps. The song is a rich warbling (not unlike a small speeded up Blackbird!). It sounds very like Garden Warbler, but is generally more varied and less rhythmic. The call is a hard "tac", very like a Lesser Whitethroat. Although most of our Blackcaps are summer visitors, increasing numbers are beginning to winter, often in gardens. It is thought that most of these are, in fact, continental birds rather than British breeders. Blackcaps become scarcer in the north and west, but otherwise breed in woods, often singing from high in the trees. but descending to brambles and undergrowth to actually build their nests. They tend to nest rather higher than Garden Warblers, and are rarely seen on the ground.

**Female** (below). Blackcaps also turn to feeding on elder, ivy and blackberries in autumn. They are increasingly seen at garden feeding stations in winter.

Sings usually from cover. The song is surprisingly rich, sweet and fruity, like a small Blackbird!

Male in breeding plumage has glossy black cap. Female shows chestnut-brown cap. Juveniles are like females, but by autumn young males may already be developing a dark cap.

VERY SIMILAR PLUMAGE TO WILLOW WARBLER, but fortunately its song gives its name away: "chiff chaff, chiff chaff". Most frequent non breeding call is "hooeet", similar to Willow Warbler, though a little more monosyllabic. Increasingly in recent years, autumn birds have been heard giving a loud "tsee u" call (the second note lower). Plumage is generally duller – browner or greyer – than Willow Warbler, and juveniles are buff rather than yellow, but there is much variation. The legs are darker than Willow Warbler, sometimes blackish. It is a fair rule to say that a black-legged bird must be a Chiffchaff, but a brown-legged bird could be either. The habitats of the two species overlap, but Chiffchaffs occur in coniferous woods that seem less liked by Willow Warblers. Both species nest on the ground. Continental migrants occur especially in late autumn, and are clearly of more eastern origin, and often look very grey and white. There is much variation amongst Chiffchaffs in Europe and Asia, and individuals often puzzle even expert birders.

The dullest Chiffchaff could perhaps be mistaken for Garden Warbler, but Chiffchaff is clearly smaller and much livelier. Often wing flicks and tail wags.

Willow Warblers and Chiffchaffs together on migration are sometimes lumped as "willowchiffs", so don't worry if you can't identify every single bird!

# WILLOW WARBLER
## 11 CM, 4.25 IN

THE COMMONEST AND MOST WIDESPREAD BRITISH SUMMER VISITOR, nesting in most parts of Britain, in a variety of habitats, including areas that have few trees (let alone Willows!). Notoriously similar in plumage to Chiffchaff, it can only be separated with certainty by measuring the primary feathers! Brown legs usually indicate a Willow Warbler, as Chiffchaffs generally have blackish legs, but you have to be really close for that! Birdwatchers sometimes even refer to migrants as Willowchiffs. Fortunately, their songs are completely different. Willow Warbler has a lovely wispy cascading phrase, going down the scale, whilst Chiffchaff sings its name! However, both species have a similar non breeding call: a soft "hoo eet". Willow Warbler rises more on the second note, but it takes a practised ear to separate them. Willow Warbler's plumage tends to be less brown (or grey) than Chiffchaff, but it is variable. Young birds can look very yellow on the underparts. (See also Wood Warbler, page 186).

➡ You will be lucky to see the leg colour, but if you do, Willow Warblers have brown legs, whilst Chiffchaff's may be brown but are usually blackish.

⬇ Yellowish underparts become paler towards autumn. **Young birds** are more yellow underneath than adults.

⬆ In spring, Willow Warblers tend to arrive a little later than Chiffchaff – they have farther to travel! They winter in tropical and southern Africa; our Chiffchaffs winter in north Africa.

# WOOD WARBLER

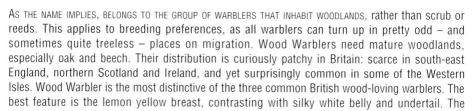

AS THE NAME IMPLIES, BELONGS TO THE GROUP OF WARBLERS THAT INHABIT WOODLANDS, rather than scrub or reeds. This applies to breeding preferences, as all warblers can turn up in pretty odd – and sometimes quite treeless – places on migration. Wood Warblers need mature woodlands, especially oak and beech. Their distribution is curiously patchy in Britain: scarce in south-east England, northern Scotland and Ireland, and yet surprisingly common in some of the Western Isles. Wood Warbler is the most distinctive of the three common British wood-loving warblers. The best feature is the lemon yellow breast, contrasting with silky white belly and undertail. The upperparts are a brighter green than the other two, and there is a conspicuous yellow stripe over the eye. The wings are particularly long, which gives the bird a short- tailed look, quite striking when seen from below. The song is most often a single wispy note repeated until it becomes a trembling sibilant trill. This is appropriately accompanied by a similarly trembling movement of the bird's whole body! The call is a loud "pee–u pee–u".

Long wings give the bird a short-tailed look, striking from below – which is often the way they are seen, as they tend to sing and feed in the canopy!

**Juvenile plumage** is duller than the adult's, but still cleaner looking and more contrasty than Willow Warbler or Chiffchaff.

The three common wood-loving warblers are Wood, Willow and Chiffchaff. All are olive above and pale below, but Wood Warbler is the most distinctive, greener than the other two.

# FIRECREST

9 CM, 3.5 IN

SCARCE IN BRITAIN, MOST FREQUENTLY SEEN ON MIGRATION – mainly at coastal locations in the south and east – but small numbers also breed in the south. Prefers mature conifers close to mixed woodlands. Looks slightly bigger than Goldcrest, probably because of its more streamlined face pattern. The white stripe over the eye is the most conspicuous feature. The upperparts are greener than Goldcrest and the underparts cleaner white. There is also a quite striking golden suffusion on the shoulder.

**Males** (left) have fireier crests than **females** (below right). **Juveniles** (above right) have no crests. Call: similar to Goldcrest's though a little rougher. Song: an evenly repeated note, accelerating on same pitch, lacking Goldcrest's trill. Note the vivid white eyebrow.

# GOLDCREST

9 CM, 3.5 IN

BRITAIN'S TINIEST BIRD, FOUND ALL OVER BRITAIN. Breeds in conifers but, in winter, visits all kinds of woods and hedgerows, including gardens. Numbers are considerably swollen by continental immigrants and – especially in October – large "falls" may occur, especially on east coast. Dark-edged wing bar is as conspicuous as crest on crown. This has an orange centre on the male, yellow on female, and is lacking in very young birds, which are most likely to be mistaken for warblers.

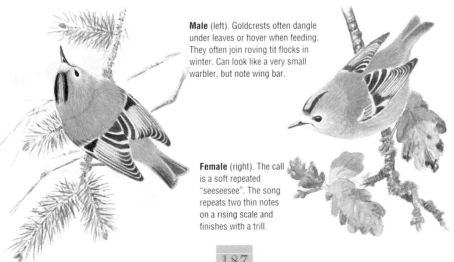

**Male** (left). Goldcrests often dangle under leaves or hover when feeding. They often join roving tit flocks in winter. Can look like a very small warbler, but note wing bar.

**Female** (right). The call is a soft repeated "seeseesee". The song repeats two thin notes on a rising scale and finishes with a trill.

# SPOTTED FLYCATCHER.

## 14 CM, 5.5 IN

SUMMER VISITOR; RARELY ARRIVES BEFORE MID-MAY OR EVEN EARLY JUNE. Breeds throughout Britain, often nesting in foliage against a tree or wall – ivy is a favourite. Also uses open nest boxes. When catching flies, it repeatedly flits off, does an acrobatic snatch, and then returns to the same or a nearby perch. Its stance is very upright. Occurs on migration at coastal locations away from trees, where it will use a rock or fence as a regular perch. Plumage is very drab: merely soft grey-brown with a few streaks on the breast and on the crown. Although the flycatching habits often attract your attention, remember that other species can also behave in a slightly similar manner. It is the upright pose and the constant returning to the same perch that tends to be the give away. Female Pied Flycatcher has the same habit, but is smaller, has no streaking, and shows white on the wing bar, and outer tail (see Pied Fly , opposite). Call is a soft high-pitched "zeee". Robins have a similar call.

Very acrobatic. Catches insects in flight, returning to a favourite perch, which is a good clue, distinguishing it from various warblers and Robins, which are pretty good at flycatching too!

Upright stance is very characteristic. Often nests in gardens, where it will take to open-fronted boxes, or build within a creeping plant such as ivy or wisteria.

**Juveniles** (right) are more speckly than the adults. Male and female look the same as each other, with soft grey-brown plumage and streaky breast.

# PIED FLYCATCHER

## 13 CM, 5 IN

SUMMER VISITOR, BREEDING IN DECIDUOUS WOODS – especially oak – in Wales, north-west England and some parts of Scotland, and very occasionally elsewhere. Nests in holes in trees, and will also readily use nest boxes. Also seen on migration at coastal locations, away from trees. Slightly smaller and neater than Spotted Flycatcher. Males in breeding plumage are unmistakably black and white. Female and juveniles (and autumn males) are dark brown above, and whitish below. They have no streaking, but show a white wing bar, and white outer tail feathers. These are conspicuous when the bird flies. Otherwise, Pied Flys can be hard to spot, as they hide under the canopy, before flitting out briefly to snatch a fly. They tend to be less addicted to favourite perches than Spotted Fly. Female Chaffinch (see page 210) is also brown with white wing bars and can be reminiscent of Pied Fly. Various calls mainly with a slightly metallic quality, including a sharp ticking. The song involves two repeated notes "zee it, zee it" with an occasional short trill.

Can be difficult to see, flitting out briefly from the canopy. Less reliant on favourite perches than Spotted Flycatcher.

**Female** and juveniles are dark brown, with whitish underparts. But if you see one in autumn, beware! - the males have moulted to become dark brown too!

**Male in breeding plumage.** Pied Flycatchers will breed in nest boxes (those with holes rather than the open-fronted kind) but often face competition for nest sites from Great Tits.

# LONG-TAILED TIT.

## 14 CM, 5.5 IN

AN EXQUISITE LITTLE BIRD, with a dumpy little body and very long tail. The plumage is pink, black and white, and it really can't be mistaken for anything else. The Long-tailed Tit builds lovely little lichen-ball nests, woven together with spider-webs (which give it a wonderful elastic quality to house a growing brood of up to twelve chicks!). They breed deep in hedges and low cover, in most parts of Britain. Out of the breeding season, they often visit gardens, but rarely come onto the nut bags so beloved of other tits. They are frequently seen in parties: usually half a dozen or so, but sometimes many more, especially if they are with other tits. It's a pretty safe rule that if you see one Long-tailed Tit, others will soon follow! The call is a high pitched "see see see", similar to Goldcrest, but on a slightly lower pitch, and they also make other low short trilling sounds. The juveniles have dingier heads than adults.

Almost always in family parties: if you see one, look for more. Feeds mainly on insects, but also seeds and buds, but not really a birdtable bird.

Pink lollipop birds – Long-tailed Tits teeter and swing on twigs, toppling slowly over like one of those balancing acrobat toys.

Pink and black and white plumage with that long tail is unmistakable. It looks rather like a mobile powder puff. Juveniles have dingier heads.

# BEARDED TIT

16.5 CM, 6.5 IN

FOUND ONLY IN REEDBEDS, MAINLY IN EAST ANGLIA AND THE SOUTH-EAST. Its alternative – and better – name is Bearded Reedling. Plump-bodied and long-tailed, nothing else this shape lives in reedbeds! Both sexes are a rich orangey above, with blackish marks on the wings, but the male has a wonderful powder blue head and smart black moustaches. Unfortunately, this isn't an easy bird to get a good view of. They usually betray their presence by calling: a ringing "ching ching", like tiny bells. They sometimes then flit rather feebly across the reed tops, before quickly flopping back into cover. Your best bet is to watch a channel between the reeds on a calm day, and wait for birds to make the crossing. They will sometimes shin up the reeds, and look around before they flutter across. Some winters, small parties of birds wander to smaller reedbeds, away from the usual breeding haunts, but they are never common. Most of their strongholds are at well known bird reserves.

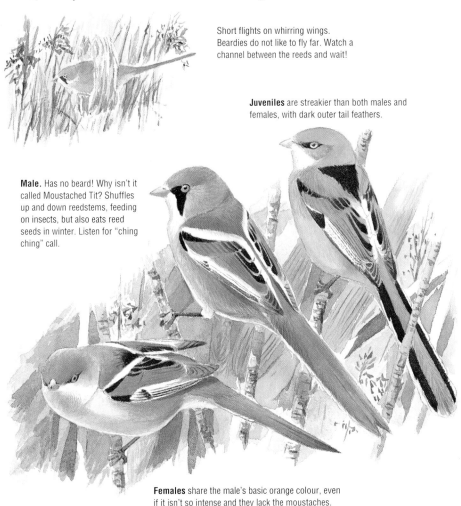

Short flights on whirring wings. Beardies do not like to fly far. Watch a channel between the reeds and wait!

**Juveniles** are streakier than both males and females, with dark outer tail feathers.

**Male.** Has no beard! Why isn't it called Moustached Tit? Shuffles up and down reedstems, feeding on insects, but also eats reed seeds in winter. Listen for "ching ching" call.

**Females** share the male's basic orange colour, even if it isn't so intense and they lack the moustaches.

# MARSH TIT

## 11.5 CM, 4.5 IN

MARSH AND WILLOW TIT ARE EXTREMELY SIMILAR, so much so that even expert birdwatchers sometimes confuse them. Both are resident in woods in England, Wales and southern Scotland. Neither is exclusively dependent on the wet habitat implied by their names. In fact, Marsh Tit in particular may occur in drier areas. They very rarely visit gardens, and are unusual visitors to bird tables. Compared with Willow, Marsh Tit is slightly less bull-necked, has a glossy black cap (dull in Willow) and a smaller black bib. Juveniles have a dull sooty black cap like Willow. Its most distinctive call is an explosive "pitchoo". Other buzzier scolding calls are more difficult to distinguish from Willow Tit. Both Marsh and Willow, lack the white nape or wing bars of Coal Tit (see page 196). Nests in holes in trees. Feeds on insects and seeds, especially beechmast.

Usually rears a single brood in a hole in a tree, such as birch or alder. Strongly territorial and aggressive.

Shiny black cap and less bull-necked appearance are best indicators from Willow Tit.

Note neat black bib. Willow's is a bit bigger. Wing uniform, lacking pale patch of Willow Tit.

# WILLOW TIT

11.5 CM, 4.5 IN

VERY SIMILAR TO MARSH TIT. In fact, Willow was not differentiated from Marsh Tit in Britain until the beginning of the twentieth century. Resident in damp woodlands in England, Wales and southern Scotland. Unlike Marsh Tit, it excavates its own nest holes, which is probably why it prefers damper areas with rotting wood. The plumage is very similar to Marsh Tit, but Willow Tit is slightly more bull-necked, the black crown is dull (not shiny), the black bib is a little larger, and there is often (but not always) a frosty pale patch on the closed wing. The most characteristic call is a nasal repeated "chair chair". Other buzzy calls are less easy to separate from Marsh Tit. Both Willow and Marsh Tit lack the white nape or wing bars of Coal Tit. Note also that male Blackcap (page 183) is basically brownish with a black cap, but is larger, slower in its movements, and lacks white cheeks or a black bib. (It is, of course, actually a warbler!)

Has more bull-necked appearance than Marsh Tit. Sooty black cap (not shiny as in Marsh) and wider black bib.

Broad bib, dull head, white cheeks and pale underparts.

Note frosty pale patch on wing. Not all birds show this patch and it is not always easy to see. Most useful feature is characteristic call.

The Willow Tit digs out a nesting chamber in rotting wood such as birch or alder, but may be evicted by more aggressive Marsh Tit.

# BLUE TIT

## 11.5 CM, 4.5 IN

WELL KNOWN AND WELL LOVED. A widespread breeding bird all over Britain, that often uses nest boxes, as well as holes and crevices in just about anything! Very familiar in gardens, where it readily comes to bird tables and ingenious feeding contraptions, as well as testing its own ingenuity by pecking through milk bottle tops to get at the cream, and removing putty from window fixings. No other bird has its blue crown, white face with black eyeline look. Juveniles are duller, with a yellow wash on the face. They are extremely active and agile in pursuit of food , especially when they are feeding their broods, which can number ten or more. Mortality is high, but the large families (up to 14 eggs are laid) mean the species survives at a healthy level, and numbers soon build up after a harsh winter. The call is a thin "see see" (less rhythmic than either Goldcrest or Long-tailed Tit) and the song is similarly sibilant and includes a trembly little trill.

**Adults** (below) have bright blue crown, white face with black eyestripe. As with other tit species, the sexes are alike but with both at the birdtable you might notice a difference in brightness.

**Juveniles** (above) are duller than the adults, the white on the face replaced by a yellow wash. Tits usually rear only one brood per year, but make it a large one!

# GREAT TIT

## 14 CM, 5.5 IN

ALMOST AS FAMILIAR AS BLUE TIT, but absent or scarce in the Highlands of Scotland and the Northern Isles. Nearly as big as a House Sparrow, and perhaps even more aggressive. Often chases other tits off the feeders. The most obvious features are the white cheeks, on an otherwise shiny black head, and the black stripe down the yellow chest (broader in males). The most similar species is Coal Tit (see Coal Tit) which also has white cheeks, but also has a white nape (back of the neck), is fawn below and is considerably smaller. Great Tits make all sorts of noises, some of them very loud and sounding almost electronic! These include a sharp "chink chink", and a repeated "teecher teecher". Great Tit's repertoire is so diverse that birdwatchers often say that if they can't recognize a woodland call, it's probably a Great Tit! Nests in holes and nest boxes.

**Young** Great Tits are duller and more washed out than adults.

**Female** Great Tits (right) feed on beechmast in winter. In a good mast year, many survive the winter; in poor years many die.

**Male** Great Tit can be distinguished from female by broad black band extending the length of the belly. Like Blue Tit, a frequent winter visitor to bird tables.

# COAL TIT

## 11.5 CM, 4.5 IN

A WIDESPREAD BREEDING SPECIES, found more in conifers than the other common tit species, but occurs in broadleaf woodland too. Also joins roving tit flocks out of the breeding season and will visit garden feeders. However, it seems much shyer than Blue or Great Tit, often nipping in, grabbing a peanut, and dashing away, probably to store it somewhere. For this reason, it may seem scarcer than it really is. Small and neat (slightly smaller than Blue Tit). It has white cheeks on a black head – a bit like a Great Tit – but also has a white nape (back of neck). The underparts vary from buffish to off-white. The whitish areas are yellower in juveniles. The call is a shrill "tsuueee", and the song a high-pitched repeated "teechu teechu teechu". Both Marsh and Willow Tit have a rather similar fawn-bodied, black-headed look, but neither has the white nape, or extended black chinstrap. They also lack the Coal Tit's white wing bars.

Adult Coal Tits in Ireland have a yellowy wash on the cheeks and nape, with buffier upperparts and a yellower flush to the underparts..

Broad white stripe at nape makes an **adult** Coal Tit look like a little Mohican! White wing bars help to separate it quickly from Marsh and Willow Tits.

The colours on the **juvenile** (below) are more subdued

# NUTHATCH

## 14 CM, 5.5 IN

RESIDENT IN MATURE WOODLAND IN ENGLAND AND WALES, but scarce in Scotland and absent from Ireland. Looks and behaves like a colourful little woodpecker, but in fact belongs to its very own family. Climbs up and down tree trunks and along branches. Can be hard to spot, but will also sometimes visit garden feeders, and be charmingly conspicuous. Nests in holes in trees, which it customizes by plastering the opening with mud, which sets like concrete!. The bird's presence in woodland is often betrayed by its calls, which include loud "kwiks" and thin "sees". Its song is a ringing repeated "peepeepeepee" (similar to Lesser Spotted Woodpecker or Kestrel, but not quite as hard-edged as either). The only other small bird that has similar plumage is male Wheatear (see page 167), but Wheatears have totally different habits, since they much prefer open ground and certainly don't climb trees! Nuthatches will also latch onto roving tit flocks.

The distinctive short black tail with white outside notches can be a useful indicator when the bird flies away. Stocky, bullet-shaped bird.

Blue-grey with apricot underparts, the Nuthatch is conspicuous when it visits bird tables. In the field, it climbs down treetrunks as easily as it climbs up them.

# TREECREEPER
## 12.5 CM, 5 IN

RESIDENT IN WOODS THROUGHOUT BRITAIN, and really quite numerous, but sometimes frustratingly hard to see! It entirely lives up to its name, by creeping, almost like a hesitant little mouse, up tree trunks and along branches. It almost invariably seems to be on the other side! It generally works its way up, then flits to the bottom of another trunk, and starts to spiral upwards again. The streaky brown upperparts provide beautiful camouflage against the brown bark. In fact, it is the gleaming white underparts that are most likely to catch your eye. The call is a thin "seeee seeee", so high-pitched that some people simply can't hear it. The song is similarly thin, but actually quite catchy: a repeated "see see", accelerating and ending with a little flourish "sissi see". It nests in cavities in tree trunks, or behind loose bark. Will often tag along with roving tit flocks out of the breeding season.

Flies from top of one tree to the base of another to start on the upward climb again.

Nests usually behind a flap of bark or crevice in a tree trunk. Also roosts in cavity in soft bark.

Uses its thin, tweezer-like bill to prise under bark and probe into it for insects. Unlike Nuthatch, does not climb *down* trunks. Tail feathers strengthened like a woodpeckers'.

# GREAT GREY SHRIKE

24 CM, 9.5 IN

THE OTHER "REGULAR" SHRIKE IN BRITAIN (see Red-backed Shrike, page 234), but in fact, a pretty rare bird. A few migrants appear – mainly in October and November and occasionally in May – and a small number winter from Europe, usually on heathlands, mainly in the south and east. Larger than Red-backed Shrike. Pale grey above, white below and with a black mask, with white wing flashes in flight and a long tail with white edges. The sexes look similar, though female and juvenile have faint grey bars on breast. Like all shrikes, tends to perch on wires and tops of bushes, and can be very conspicuous, constantly flicking tail. However, despite this, it is perfectly possible to wander a heathland all day without seeing a Great Grey that you know is there somewhere! Shrikes are famous for their unsavoury habits of impaling prey on thorns, saving it in a "larder" to eat later. The Great Grey is large enough to take small birds and mammals, as well as insects.

Lengthy flights tend to be undulating: short ones between perches tend to be low to the ground, sweeping upwards at the last moment.

**Male.** Upright stance is typical, together with tail continually flicking up and down, as it watches and waits for prey such as a mouse, which it catches by a downward swoop.

**Female** (above). Slightly hooked bill betrays the shrike's predatory habits. A bird of heathland, it perches on conspicuous posts, but may be very difficult to catch sight of.

# JAY
## 34 CM, 13.5 IN

A FAMILIAR BIRD TO MOST PEOPLE, and yet one that is often the cause of confusion, or at least surprise. Resident in many parts of Britain, and often visits parks and gardens. However, its habits are fairly secretive, and therefore its vivid colours often seem to cause a bit of a shock. Reports of rare and exotic birds often turn out to be just Jays. Different bits, seem to catch different eyes – the crest, the blue flash on the wing, or the vivid white rump when it flies and, of course, the salmon pink body, which can look very bright in sunlight. All bits of the same undeniably handsome bird! The flight style is rather bounding, on rounded wings. The only species that is really confusable is the rare Hoopoe (see page 231) which is also pink, black and white, but is actually very distinctive.

White rump, black tail and blue and white wing flashes make an encounter with a Jay quite startling. Jays enjoy bathing; puddles on a road may tempt one into the open.

Jays make a ghastly noise: a harsh screeching, which invariably panics all the other birds in the garden, with good reason, since Jays readily feed on nestlings and eggs.

In autumn Jays turn to acorns. They eat some, bury a lot more, presumably for later, and are reckoned to be important agents in the spread of oak trees.

# MAGPIE

## 46 CM, 18 IN

A VERY FAMILIAR BIRD, AND BECOMING EVEN MORE SO, as numbers appear to be increasing, though it is still scarce in northern Scotland. Because it takes nestlings and eggs – and is very conspicuous when doing so – it has become the target of some distrust – not to say dislike! However, there is little evidence that Magpies are seriously depleting the numbers of our songbirds. The decline in certain species is far more to do with habitat loss and pesticides and so on, (not to mention cats!). Magpies are in fact very intelligent and handsome birds, their pied plumage having a metallic gloss. They are also pretty unmistakable. The call is a chattering "chack chacking". They build large domed nests, made out of twigs, towards the tops of trees. Out of the breeding season, they are often seen in parties – sometimes known as Magpie weddings – and even larger numbers may gather at winter roosts.

Direct in flight. Note long diamond-shaped tail, often in pairs or small family parties, following one behind another.

**Young** Magpies (above) have short tails. The Magpie population has increased substantially now that there are fewer keepered estates. Note large, football-shaped nest.

On the ground it walks and when excited lurches and hops in crabwise fashion. Close views reveal the glossy metallic gleam especially on the tail.

# JACKDAW

## 33 CM, 13 IN

CONSIDERABLY SMALLER THAN ROOK OR CROW, and with a largely grey head, contrasting with the sooty black of the rest of the bird. The white eye is set off by a darker face. Breeds widely in Britain, but is absent or scarce in some areas. Colonies often favour old ruins, quarries and sea cliffs, as well as old or dead trees, and also church towers, or even down disused chimneys. In certain areas it's a familiar sight in towns, whereas the other black crows are much more "country" birds. The call is a short "chack" (from which it gets its name), and a slightly more echoey "keeow". The most similar species is the rare Chough (see page 235). A closer view will soon reveal the differences, but they can also be distinguished in flight by the Chough's more ragged-looking wing tips, and its higher pitched more sneezing call. Jackdaws often join other crows (corvids) in mixed feeding flocks in winter.

White eye, grey head and nape, contrast with sooty plumage. Jackdaw walks with quick, jaunty strides, less sedate than either Carrion Crow or Rook. Also flies faster with quicker wingbeats.

Jackdaws nest in holes, in ruins, quarries, old tree trunks, that's why they often find chimneys make very convenient nest-sites!

# RAVEN
## 64 CM, 25 IN

THE LARGEST OF THE BLACK CROWS BY FAR, but this isn't always immediately appreciated unless other species are present for comparison. Ravens are found only in western Britain and Ireland, and only near sea cliffs and upland craggy areas, though they will feed on farmland and even refuse tips. They build a nest of sticks and twigs on cliffs and crags, and sometimes trees. The head is particularly large, with a big, deep bill, and a shaggy throat. In flight, Raven's tail is noticeably wedge-shaped, wings often with primaries spread into open "fingers". Ravens are most often seen singly, or in pairs, or small parties – but they will gather in larger groups at roost, although not in the large flocks of Crow or Rook. Pairs often tumble and roll in mid-air during their display flight. They are very agile in the air and seem to enjoy playing in the wind. Imposing, even at a distance, Ravens have a very gruff, deep croaking call.

Compare **Raven's** big-headed, wedge-tailed look with **Rook** (far left) and **Carrion Crow** (centre). All these crows can be acrobatic in flight, but the Raven's tumbling and rolling is particularly impressive.

Shaggy throat feathers and huge bill make the Raven's profile distinctive. It feeds on carrion as well as small mammals, birds and molluscs as well as vegetable matter.

# ROOK
## 46 CM, 18 IN

BREEDS THROUGHOUT BRITAIN, ALWAYS IN COLONIES, known of course as rookeries. The nests are conspicuous, built in the top of tall trees. Otherwise, feeds on farmland, and rarely comes into truly built up areas. Very similar to Carrion Crow, but Rook is slightly smaller and less stockily built, the crown of the head is noticeably peaked, the bill is more dagger-shaped and is whitish (though young Rooks have dark bills). The feathering at the top of the legs is also shaggier, like a pair of feathery shorts. The flight silhouette is also subtly different from Crow, with slimmer wings, a slightly longer more rounded tail, and faster wingbeats. The call is "caar", less croaky and more echoey than Carrion Crow. Feeds much more on grain and vegetable matter than Carrion Crow, but will also take invertebrates, small mammals and carrion. Often feeds in flocks, sometimes very large ones.

Folklore would have it that if the rooks build at the tops of trees, the spring and summer will be fine. Elms used to be favoured sites.

**Juveniles** (above) have dark feathered beak and are more clean-legged than the adults – compare with Carrion Crow. They take two years to reach maturity.

**Adult** Rooks at close range easily told from Carrion Crow by large, whitish bill, and shaggy "trousers". Crown is more peaked. Has a swaggering walk on the ground, occasionally hops.

# CARRION CROW/HOODED CROW

### 47 CM, 18.5 IN

THERE ARE FIVE SPECIES OF BLACK "CROWS" IN BRITAIN. Carrion Crows are found throughout the British Isles, but are replaced in Ireland and north and western Scotland by the race known as Hooded Crow. This is, in fact, very easy to recognize with its grey body, and black hood and wings. Carrion Crow (the all black form) is most similar to Rook and Raven (see pages 203 and 204). Raven is much bigger. Rook has a white bill, and steeper forehead. It used to be said that if you saw a flock of Crows in a field, they were Rooks, but this doesn't really make sense. Crows can gather in large winter feeding flocks and at roosts. However, they do not breed in colonies like Rooks. The call is a croaking "craw", but it also produces variations, some of which sound strangely hollow, almost comical. They are common in town parks, where Rooks would rarely wander. Nests in trees, but also on cliff ledges.

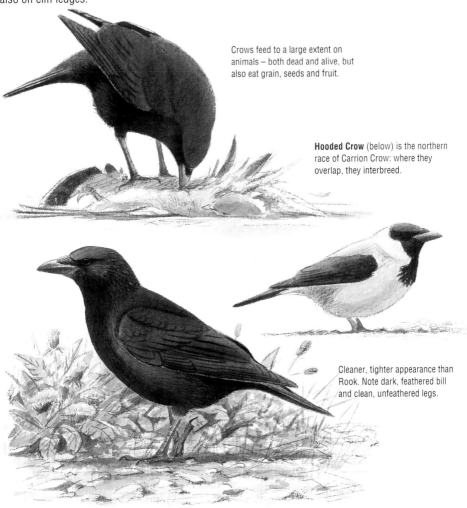

Crows feed to a large extent on animals – both dead and alive, but also eat grain, seeds and fruit.

**Hooded Crow** (below) is the northern race of Carrion Crow: where they overlap, they interbreed.

Cleaner, tighter appearance than Rook. Note dark, feathered bill and clean, unfeathered legs.

# HOUSE SPARROW

## 14.5 CM, 5.75 IN

A FAMILIAR AND WIDESPREAD RESIDENT, usually in the vicinity of buildings of some kind, even if it's only derelict farms or ruins. The male is very distinctive, only confusable with Tree Sparrow. Note that House Sparrow has grey centre to the crown (all brown in Tree Sparrow), and has larger and messier black bib, and no cheek spot. Female and juvenile House Sparrows are much duller and, with a poor view, can be confused with juvenile Greenfinch (see page 212). Stray birds in odd places – for example, skulking in low cover on a coastal headland – have caused birdwatchers to hope for something rarer on more than one occasion! House Sparrows nest in a variety of places, including holes in trees or buildings, or even build an untidy nest in a hedge. They chirrup rather than sing, though they can string a number of chirrups together when they are displaying or agitated.

In winter even the **male** House Sparrow (above) loses its colours, the crown and bib becoming flecked with white.

**Male.** As well as nesting under the eaves of houses, House Sparrows will also take over old House Martin nests, or build in the lower structure of larger nests.

**Female** and **juvenile** House Sparrows are the archetypal little dull brown birds, lacking the male's dark bib and head markings. They can be confused with young Greenfinches.

# TREE SPARROW
## 14 CM, 5.75 IN

BECOMING INCREASINGLY SCARCE, probably due to loss of habitat to modern farming methods. Nevertheless, it still breeds in various parts of Britain, though it is rare in north Scotland. Forms small flocks out of the breeding season, but these involve far fewer birds than twenty or thirty years ago. A good place to look for them is in farm stockyards, where they may join other seed-eaters on spilt grain. Both male and female have the same plumage, and even the juveniles are not as different as in most species. Rather like a smaller neater version of male House Sparrow, but note that the cap is entirely chestnut-brown (not grey centred as in House Sparrow), the bib is smaller and neater, and there is a conspicuous black cheek spot, and narrow white collar. It hardly has a song, but the call is a distinctive short sharp "tchek". Nests in holes in trees and buildings, and will sometimes take over old Sand Martin's nests, or use nest boxes meant for tits.

**Juvenile.** Much more retiring than House Sparrows, and less associated with human habitation, Tree Sparrows tend to live in open woodland, hedgerows and orchards.

**Male** and **female** Tree Sparrows have similar plumage. Neat black bib, cheek spot and rich chestnut cap separate from male House Sparrow.

# STARLING

21.5 CM, 8.5 IN

BREEDS ALL OVER BRITAIN, in holes in trees or crevices in rocks, cliffs and buildings. Large numbers arrive from the continent in autumn and spend the winter here. Forms large roosts, sometimes involving thousands of birds which fly in spectacular clouds as they come in at dusk or leave at dawn. These roosts may be in trees, reedbeds or in the centre of towns or cities. Adult Starlings may look black, but in fact their plumage is iridescent, with all colours of the rainbow, and there is extensive whitish spotting on the body feathers. Starling's song is full of scratchy whistles and trills, and often incorporates the calls of other birds, which may include Curlews and Redshanks, so accurate that they sometimes fool birdwatchers! They may also impersonate human "wolf whistles", or even phone or door bells. A migrating flock of Starlings looks rather similar to a party of Redwings (page 173), but note the triangular pointed wing shape of Starlings.

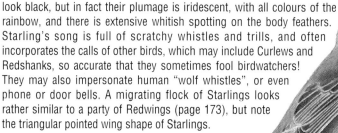

**Juvenile** (above) will run after parent bird on ground, almost treading on its heels. Starlings often feed in flocks on lawns, playing fields and farmland.

In **breeding plumage** (left), the bill is yellow and plumage looks glossy black. In winter the birds have a more spangled, spotted effect. Arrow-shaped in flight.

**Moulting plumage** (above). Juveniles are sandy brown, and in late summer the adult plumage begins to moult through, creating an odd half-and-half effect.

# BULLFINCH

14.5–16 CM, 5.75–6.25 IN

OCCURS ALL OVER BRITAIN, AND BREEDS IN WOODLAND WITH BUSHY EDGES, but is never particularly numerous or conspicuous. Its taste for the buds of fruit trees in orchards means it is sometimes considered a pest and accordingly persecuted: maybe that's why it's so shy! Usually seen in pairs or in small parties, rarely into double figures. The male's rich pink underparts are replaced by a soft fawn in the female, while youngsters at first lack the black cap. In flight, the most conspicuous feature is its white rump, which is often all you glimpse, as it slips away into the foliage. The call is a soft piping "phew", which often betrays the bird's presence, challenging you to actually see it. Some autumns, continental immigrants arrive on the east coast, and a few stay to winter, but – unlike most other small seed-eating birds – they never seem to join mixed flocks on stubble fields. Nests in thick hedges and dense evergreen shrubs.

**Juveniles** (below) lack the adults' black cap, but in flight the white rump and short conical bill are good indicators.

**Female** (right). Bullfinches usually go around in pairs, and appear to be monogamous. It is thought that they retain the same mate in successive breeding seasons, assuming both survive.

**Male** (above) looks bold in black and shocking pink, but Bullfinches are shy - not surprising considering their liking for fruit buds, though this tends to be when other seeds have failed.

# CHAFFINCH

15 CM, 6 IN

PERHAPS SURPRISINGLY, ONE OF THE COMMONEST BIRDS IN BRITAIN. Chaffinches are found in just about every type of habitat in all areas. Nevertheless they seem to be decreasing, possibly as a result of weed control on farmland, which reduces their food supply. They are, however, still common birds whose numbers are considerably swelled in winter by Scandinavian immigrants. Migrating flocks are often noticeable, especially in October, when they may travel alongside other finches, such as Bramblings, Siskins and Linnets. Brambling is similar shape and size, but is a winter visitor and much rarer. Chaffinch's song is a fruity warble, which accelerates and ends with a flourish. Its rhythm has been likened to a fast bowler running up and releasing a ball. The commonest call is a sharp ringing "pink", but they also give a loud "hooeet" (similar to both Redstart and Willow Warbler) and other short, wheezy calls. Female Chaffinches glimpsed flitting around in treetops can momentarily resemble female Pied Flycatchers (which also have white wing bars and white outer tail). Remember that Pied Flys are only summer visitors to a relatively few areas, but if you get a good view of them, you will not mistake them.

**Male** Chaffinch is very distinctive in breeding plumage, with powder-blue head, steel-blue beak and pink breast. Outside the breeding season, the beak is paler.

Double white wing bar and white outer tail feathers are conspicuous in flight. Sometimes you can see the male's greenish rump.

**Winter plumage male** On the ground, Chaffinches move with a hesitant, shuffling little hop, almost as if they are limping.

**Females** and young birds are smooth brown, with a double white wing bar, almost like a female House Sparrow, were it not for the wing bars.

# BRAMBLING

14.5 CM, 5.75 IN

THE WINTER VERSION OF THE CHAFFINCH. Variable numbers arrive in October to spend the winter in Britain. In some years, it is quite widespread, but it is always scarce in Ireland. Particularly fond of beechmast and – in a good year – large flocks may form in favoured areas. Generally though, this is a bird that you are perhaps more likely to see flying away or overhead, often in the company of Chaffinches. The most noticeable feature in flight is the white rump. Bramblings lack the white outer tail feathers of Chaffinch. The call is also very distinctive; a soft "chuck chuck" (almost inaudible) followed by a loud harsh "tsweek". I remember it as "chuckle and squeak"! Seen on the ground, it is immediately reminiscent of a Chaffinch, but notice the orange tones on the underparts and on the shoulder, and the darker streaky head pattern. In fact, breeding plumage males have black heads, but this is rarely seen in Britain, except in late spring, especially in the northern isles before birds return to Scandinavia.

In flight, note the oval-shaped white rump patch, and white wing bar.

**Males** become darker as spring approaches and the tips of their feathers wear away to reveal full breeding plumage, but this is unlikely to be seen in Britain.

**Females** have orangey tones on the underparts and on the shoulder, like males though not quite so bright, but with greyer heads.

# GREENFINCH

## 14.5 CM, 5.75 IN

COMMON ALL OVER BRITAIN, INCLUDING PARKS AND GARDENS. Numbers are swelled by continental immigrants in autumn and winter. Male Greenfinch is very distinctive. Females and juveniles are both duller and/or streakier, and can be confused with other species. Female House Sparrow (see page 206) is browner still, with a pale eyestripe. Female and juvenile Crossbills (see page 215) look very similar, and Greenfinches also tend to like fir trees, where Crossbills occur. Moreover, Greenfinch's single note flight call is also rather Crossbill-like. When you are looking for Crossbills, make sure it's not a poor view of a Greenfinch! Even the dingiest Greenfinch will show a hint of yellow along its wing and at its tail base, and they have a pale pointed bill (i.e. not crossed!). Song is rather canary-like, involving a long nasal "dzweeee". This is often delivered during a bat-like fluttery song flight. The full flight call is a distinctive one note almost trilled "tititi," but it also has a single note version, which is less easy to be sure of.

**Male** (left) and **female**. The only other green-ish finch is Siskin, but Greenfinch is clearly much bigger, with pale bill, and is largely unstreaked. A typical seed-eater, with a large conical bill.

Note yellow flash along the outer edge of the wing – not wing bars (like Siskin), also yellow at base of tail. Often forms flocks with House Sparrows, Chaffinches and buntings.

**Young birds** (left) are browner and more streaked. They could sometimes be mistaken for Crossbills, a far less common or widespread species.

# GOLDFINCH

## 12 CM, 4.75 IN

A COMMON RESIDENT IN BRITAIN, EXCEPT FOR THE FAR NORTH OF SCOTLAND. The best place to look for Goldfinches is on thistle heads, which they probe with their rather long pointy beaks. The largest flocks build up in autumn, but some of our Goldfinches then migrate farther south, and a few arrive from the continent to winter here. Male and female are very distinctive, but the juveniles lack the black, white and red face markings. Broad golden wing bar is the best feature. Siskin (see page 214) is perhaps the only small finch that can look a bit similar, but note its double wing bar, streaky plumage and overall much greener tone. Goldfinch call is a tinkly twitter, which makes them easy to pick up when flying over. The song has much the same quality, but is longer and involves a few more wheezy notes and phrases.

**Juvenile** is duller, with streaks, lacking the distinctive face markings. Wing markings, including golden wing bar, are best clue.

In flight, shows broad golden wing bar. Often calls, a tinkling twittering sound, like tiny bells.

The red face feathers are quite coarse, giving protection against sharp thistles and bristly teasels – favourite foods for the Goldfinch, whose thin, pointy beak is ideal for tweaking out seeds.

The sexes are similar. In autumn and winter, Goldfinches often join flocks with other seed-eaters, such as Greenfinches, Linnets or Sparrows.

# SISKIN
## 12 CM, 4.75 IN

BREEDS IN CONIFER WOODS, ESPECIALLY IN SCOTLAND, WALES AND IRELAND. Otherwise, mainly a winter visitor to southern regions. Look for them particularly in alder trees and, to a lesser extent, birches usually in small flocks, but sometimes up to a hundred or more. They will also feed on nut bags in gardens. In flight, the birds stay in a very close flock and have a fast bouncy style. They almost invariably call: a soft piping "tseu". The twittery song is full of canary-like wheezing: like speeded up Greenfinch! Apart from at the breeding areas, the song is sometimes heard from wintering birds on warm spring mornings. The males have the darker crowns and bibs, and they become blackest in the breeding plumage. The dullest females or juveniles look rather like Redpoll (see page 215), which favour the same habitats and tree species, but Redpoll is browner. Siskins always have a tinge of yellow somewhere, especially on the wing bars.

Yellow wing bars in flight not really as noticeable as those of Goldfinch and Greenfinch. Compare also female and juvenile Crossbill.

The **male** becomes darker as the breeding season approaches. Often quite tame little birds, Siskins will allow a close approach. They tend to breed in conifers.

Commonly feed in winter with Redpolls, on birch and alder seeds. **Females** (right) and juveniles can be confused with Redpolls.

**Juvenile** (left). Siskins are increasingly reported as garden birds, where they are attracted by bright red bags of peanuts!

# REDPOLL
### 13–15 CM, 5–6 IN

# CROSSBILL
### 16.5 CM, 6.5 IN

**REDPOLL** BREEDS ALL OVER BRITAIN, mainly in young conifer plantations. Redpoll is clearly browner than Siskins – lacking any yellow tones – with white wing bars. The males have the reddest foreheads, and may have a raspberry flush in the throat as well. Different races occur, which may look frostier in general plumage, with paler rumps. Juvenile Linnet and Twite (page 216) are similar in size and jizz to Redpolls. **Crossbills** breed exclusively in conifers, but are by no means present in all plantations. However, Crossbills are prone to "irrrupting" in some years – probably due to variable pine crops – and suddenly they will breed in a new area, only to desert it the following season.

**Female Crossbill.** Smooth dull green or almost brown; juveniles are streaked. They are not dissimilar to Greenfinches, which may occur in similar woodland and also have a short "gip " call.

**Female Redpoll** (left) and **winter male** (above). Though Redpoll was formerly commoner than Siskin, the situation recently seems to have reversed.! Flocks form in winter, especially in alders and birches.

**Adult male Crossbill** unmistakable, pink all over, though darker on the back. Young males are less red: almost as if they haven't fully ripened! Flight call: a liquid "chip chip chip".

**Male** (above) **Redpoll's** call is a slightly zingy "chi chi chi", and the song adds a cheery rattling trill to this. Both call and song are often given in flight.

# LINNET
## 13.5 CM, 5.25 IN
# TWITE
## 13.5 CM, 5.25 IN

LINNET IS RESIDENT IN MOST PARTS OF BRITAIN, except north-west Scotland, where it is replaced by Twite. Particularly partial to heathy scrubby areas with gorse, but will also breed in farmland hedges and even in tangly gardens. Also occurs on migration, when continental birds may be involved. Flocks out of the breeding season often join with other seed-eaters on rough ground, stubble or saltmarshes. Linnet's flight call is a dry twittering that is surprisingly easy to get to know and recognize. The song incorporates this twitter, along with various wheezy calls and whistles. **Twite** is very much the highland version of the Linnet, but by no means present on all uplands in Britain. Has a rather limited distribution: in the Pennines, in Scotland and on the west coast of Ireland. Small numbers also winter at certain favoured locations in the south. Flight call: "cheweet" – a little more explosive and drawn out than Linnet's. Song rather similar to Linnet but twangier. Nest in heather, crevices in rocks or stone walls.

**Male Linnet** (above) has red flush on its head and breast that make it look as if it has been dipped in raspberry juice.

**Female Linnet** (top) and juvenile have streaked upperparts and flanks. Best identification feature is frosty white wing flashes: a feature shown by none of the other small streaky finches.

**Male** and **female Twite** are the same: small, brown and streaky, with a pale yellowish bill in winter (dark in summer). Males in breeding plumage may show a slightly pink rump.

# HAWFINCH

18 CM, 7 IN

A LARGE STRIKING FINCH, THAT IS NEVERTHELESS EXTREMELY DIFFICULT TO SEE. Resident in woodlands – with a particular liking for Hornbeams and cherry orchards -mainly in England, and a few parts of Wales and southern Scotland. Absent from Ireland. Your best chance of seeing one is probably to hear its call, and then catch a glimpse as it – or they – flit across the top of the canopy. The call is a sharp "tzik", similar to a Robin (but Robins don't often venture to the very tops of woodland trees). While searching for Hawfinches, briefly glimpsed Chaffinches will often lead you astray, as they too flash white wing bars, but – as with so many scarce birds- the rule is that when you see it, you'll know! Hawfinches really are very handsome indeed, and well worth the patience required to see them. A few migrants occur, usually in October, and may then even appear in relatively treeless areas at the coast, but they won't stop long!

The flight jizz is very short-tailed and large-headed. It shows broad white flashes on the upperwing and – uniquely – a white tip to the tail.

**Male** (foreground) and **female**. Generally feeds at the top of the woodland canopy. Huge bill (grey-blue in the breeding season; yellowish at other times) can crack cherry stones: beechmast and Hornbeam seeds are important foods.

# SNOW BUNTING

## 16.5 CM, 6.5 IN

A FEW PAIRS BREED ON THE ALMOST INACCESSIBLE MOUNTAIN TOPS OF SCOTLAND. Otherwise, it is a winter visitor from the Arctic Circle, occurring from September to April mainly at coastal locations, especially in the north and east. They feed in tight flocks, creeping along short turf, stubble or shingly seashores, the rear birds periodically fluttering to overtake those at the front and – when they fly – they really do resemble a brief snow flurry. On the ground, they can look surprisingly unstriking, as there are usually far more females and juveniles than males. In fact the lovely breeding plumage male is only likely to be seen on the breeding grounds, or as a very late spring migrant. Nevertheless, no other finch-like bird is so white on the underparts, face and wings. The upperparts have a distinct gingery tinge to them. The call is an appropriate jingly twittering, and they also have a ringing "teeu", that is similar to a Lapland Bunting (see page 235) but a little more drawn out.

Flying flocks really do resemble a flurry of snow. Usually seen in small flocks of fewer than 50 birds. Numbers wintering in Britain vary considerably.

**Female.** Look for Snow Buntings in autumn and winter around the coast, on short-grass fields, rough land and shingly beaches. In winter, they feed principally on seeds.

Long-winged for a bunting, **male** becomes progressively whiter as spring approaches. White wing patches and underparts always very distinctive. Variable amount of white on face.

218

# CORN BUNTING

## 18 CM, 7 IN

THE LARGEST AND – IT HAS TO BE SAID – CLUMSIEST LOOKING OF THE BUNTINGS. Almost striking in its lack of obvious markings! Both sexes and all ages are dull brown, with streaking above and below, but no clear wing bars or face pattern. It doesn't even have white outer tail feathers! Often conspicuously perched on a post or wires, where its large yellowy bill and pink legs are noticeable. Its song is a scratchy jangle, likened to a bunch of keys being shaken. The flight call is a short liquid "kwit". Corn Buntings are well distributed on arable farmland across much of England, but are scarce or absent in the south-west, Wales, Ireland and most of Scotland (except some parts of the east and Outer Hebrides). This patchy distribution is likely to get even patchier, as they seem to be generally declining, probably due to modern farming methods. In winter, quite large flocks may be seen and heard flying to their roosts. Less inclined to join mixed species flocks than other buntings and finches.

Very sedentary and predictable during the breeding season, males can be found on the same songposts day after day. When they take off, Corn Buntings trail their long, pale legs.

A large bunting, both **male** and **female** are dull brown with streaks. The male's jangly song is probably the most conspicuous feature of this farmland bird.

# YELLOWHAMMER

16.5 CM, 6.5 IN

RESIDENT ALL OVER BRITAIN, MAINLY IN OPEN COUNTRY, with nearby hedgerows and areas of scrub. The males can be very conspicuous during the early breeding season, when they perch on top of bushes and sing their famous "little bit o' bread and no cheeeese" song. This is, in fact, only the rhythm: the tone is quite thin and metallic, ending with the long drawn-out wheeeze (the "cheeeese" bit!). Females and juveniles look very similar to female or juvenile Cirl Bunting (see page 235). Remember though that Cirl Bunting is a very rare and localized bird. Yellowhammer has a chestnut rump, whereas Cirl Bunting's is brown. Female or juvenile Reed Bunting is also brown and streaky, but has rufous cheeks and a rufous shoulder patch. The flight calls are a metallic "chip", and a soft "tillip".

In flight, the rather long tail and white outer tail feathers are noticeable, as is the bright chestnut rump when the bird takes off in front of you. (Note that several other species also have white outer tail: other buntings, Chaffinches, and larks and pipits.)

**Juvenile** (above). Out of breeding season, Yellowhammers may well join mixed feeding flocks, along with other finches and buntings.

**Female** (right). Yellowhammers usually nest at the base of hedges or bushes, often on the ground, the nest partly hidden by grass. It feeds on the ground, but often sings from a tree.

**Adult males** (above) are very yellow indeed, but females and young birds can be rather brown and dull, with the yellow restricted merely to a wash on the face pattern.

# REED BUNTING

### 15 CM, 6 IN

COMMON RESIDENT ALL OVER BRITAIN. By no means only seen in reeds, although it does often breed near water. In winter, it may join other species in mixed flocks of finches and buntings. The male has a black head and bib with a white moustache. Females and juveniles are – inevitably – less boldly marked, being dark brown above, with a lot of streaking, as are males in winter. The features that distinguish Reed Bunting from similar streaky buntings are the rufous cheek, outlined in black, and the small rufous patch at the shoulder (Compare Yellowhammer, Cirl and Lapland Buntings). Like several species, they have white outer tail feathers, but these are perhaps even more vivid in Reed Bunting due to its habit of flicking its tail as it drops into cover. The commonest flight calls are a plaintive thin "tseeee u", and a loud "tsik". The song is short and neat: "chink chink chink chittichink", accelerating into the last phrase. Usually delivered from a bush or reed top perch.

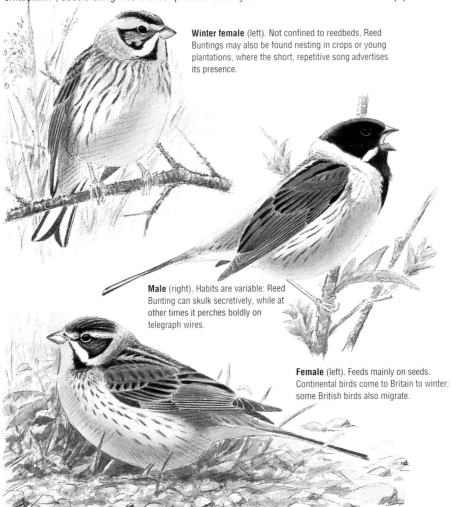

**Winter female** (left). Not confined to reedbeds, Reed Buntings may also be found nesting in crops or young plantations, where the short, repetitive song advertises its presence.

**Male** (right). Habits are variable: Reed Bunting can skulk secretively, while at other times it perches boldly on telegraph wires.

**Female** (left). Feeds mainly on seeds. Continental birds come to Britain to winter: some British birds also migrate.

# SIMILAR SPECIES:
# LITTLE BROWN BIRDS

SKULKERS AND WARBLER "IMPERSONATORS". Wren, Dunnock and Robin: these three have all been responsible for many a claim of a "possible" rare warbler. They can all creep and skulk and give only tantalizing glimpses. Robins are particularly versatile, often flicking like chats or fluttering like flycatchers. If you think you are in pursuit of a rarity, ask yourself are you sure it isn't just a shy or poorly seen common species?

**Wren**
A quick flash of its eyestripe can look very warbler-like.

**Sedge Warbler**
A true eye-striped warbler.

**Dunnock**
Often shows just a flick of its wings or tail.

**Robin**
Much less distinctive if seen from behind or in flight. The red breast isn't always obvious.

**Juvenile Stonechat**
Scaly, with odd patches of orange. Another question worth asking yourself if a bird's plumage doesn't quite seem to fit the book: is it in moult?

**Male Redstart**
Can look messy like this in both spring and – especially – in autumn. In many species both juveniles and adults in "intermediate" plumages can look scruffy, and therefore confusing.

**Young Robin**
Red breast only partially developed. This common species may bear a passing resemblance to rare species, so beware!

**Lapland Bunting**
The first step to identification is to make sure what family the bird belongs to, in this case the buntings.

**Female Yellowhammer**
Small birds may shuffle around obscured by stubble or short grass.

**Tree Sparrow**
Some birds show patches of colour or blackish markings.

**Skylark**
If you can see the bill shape, that will be a good start to pinpointing the correct family.

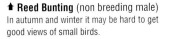

**Reed Bunting** (non breeding male)
In autumn and winter it may be hard to get good views of small birds.

**Meadow Pipit**
Is the bird smooth or streaky.

# RARE, ESCAPED AND LOCALIZED BIRDS

THE FOLLOWING PAGES SHOW A NUMBER OF SPECIES that are rare, or have most probably escaped from captivity. Some of them are – fortunately – pretty easy to identify, but others can be confused with commoner species.

Wildfowl collections often include not only "exotic" ducks and geese, but also species that do occasionally occur in Britain as genuine rarities. A few tell-tale signs may lead you to be suspicious of a bird's credentials. Is it unusually tame? Is it sporting a ring on its leg? Do the tips of its wings look cut short – (evidence of wing clipping)? Or is it the middle of summer? (Most genuine rare wildfowl occur in winter). Even if the bird looks and acts as if it is wild, I'm afraid that's not proof that it really is. Maybe it doesn't matter if it's good to look at! These initial pages include only some of the suspicious wildfowl that you may well see.

### Bar-headed Goose
This will always definitely be an escape – the species belongs in India. Fortunately, it is not really confusable with any genuine British geese.

### Swan Goose
A farmyard goose that has gone astray. May interbreed with Greylags. The give-away is usually the saggy belly!

### Wood Duck
A native of America – an escape. Similar looks and habits to Mandarin (page 31). **Male** (below left) lacks Mandarin's "sails", but the female really is very similar. Hope there's a pair of them!

### Muscovy Duck
Another farmyard wanderer which may join wild ducks, but they are usually tame and dozy, and the weird shape is unmistakable. Also occurs in black and white.

### Chiloe Wigeon
A frequent escapee. Does not occur wild. Similar shape to Wigeon (see page 32) but male has different head colours. Females are so similar you wouldn't notice them anyway!

## Snow Goose
Wild Snow Geese are found among flocks of other wild geese (usually Greenland Whitefronts), mainly in Scotland or Ireland. Snow Geese farther south are probably escapes. Snow Geese in summer certainly are.

## Ferruginous Duck
Very rarely a genuine wild bird. Same kind of inland waters as Tufted and Pochard. Beware female Tufteds with white undertails, and hybrids between Tufted and Pochard, or even with Ferruginous.

## Red-breasted Goose
A very few genuine wild birds probably occur; those found with flocks of Brent, Pinkfeet or Whitefronts probably have the best credentials. However, it is very common in captivity and undoubtedly escapes.

## Red-crested Pochard
**Female** (left) and **male** (right). More likely to be an escape than a genuinely wild bird. Seen on park lakes, ponds and reservoirs. Beware confusing female with female Ruddy Duck, Smew or Common Scoter(see pages 40, 45 and 46).

## Ruddy Shelduck
Either an extreme rarity or – far more likely – a fairly common escape from collections. Largely apricot coloured, with large white wing patches. Most confusable with Egyptian Goose.

## Egyptian Goose
A weird-looking bird that looks more like a large exotic duck than any of the British geese. Not a wild species, but a feral population has built up in East Anglia, and is now accepted on the British list.

### Bean Goose
A rare species only found in small numbers
in one or two favoured locations in
Scotland and East Anglia, and it is only
there that you are really likely to see them.

### King Eider (male)
A few occur each year, almost exclusively off the coast of
Scotland or the Northern Isles, sometimes – not always –
with Common Eiders. This is a **male**.

### Surf Scoter
**Female** (left) and **male** (right). Not kept in captivity.
A few occur each winter, mainly off Scottish or Irish
coasts, usually among flocks of the commoner
Scoter species – see pages 46–47 for comparison.
Like Velvet Scoter with all dark wing.

### Spoonbill
Most likely at one of the east coast bird reserves
(e.g. Minsmere in Suffolk or Cley in Norfolk) in
spring or autumn. A few also occur in winter,
mainly on southern estuaries.

### Little Egret
Rare until the last ten years, has become
increasingly common. Most likely on an
estuary or marsh in the southern half of
England, though has been recorded in
most areas.

### White-tailed Eagle
Reintroduction programme in the Western
Isles (Hebrides): a few young have been
successfully reared. More likely on the
ground than Golden; when it takes off it is
like a flying barn door!

### Honey Buzzard
Much rarer than Buzzard. Just a few pairs at
well known but well protected sites in the
southern half of England. Summer visitor.
Very variable. Soars on flatter wings than
Common Buzzard (see page 60).

### Rough-legged Buzzard
A winter visitor only, almost exclusively to the
east coast. Just a few may also pass through
the Northern Isles or Scotland in spring on their
way to Scandinavian breeding grounds.

### Golden Eagle
Biggest native British bird of prey
(introduced White-Tailed Sea Eagles are
even bigger!). Only in highlands of Scotland
and the Western Isles (plus a lone pair in
the Lake District). Beware confusion with
–much commoner – Buzzard. When you
really see an Eagle, you'll know!

**Lady Amherst's Pheasant** (foreground)
Yet another exotic that hardly qualifies as a wild bird but there are a few pretending in southern woodlands. Male dazzlingly obvious. Female similar to Golden Pheasant but larger.

**Golden Pheasant**
An exotic introduction. Small numbers almost wild in East Anglia, Galloway and the Isles of Scilly, and they might establish elsewhere. Despite **male's** (left) gaudy plumage, a shy species.

**Kentish Plover**
A rare but annual visitor to Britain in small numbers, most likely in spring and autumn. Similar coastal habitat to Ringed Plover. Resembles juvenile Ringed Plover (page 81), but note black legs.

**Pectoral Sandpiper**
The most frequent American species to occur this side of the Atlantic. Mainly recorded in September or October especially in Ireland. Usually skulks in low vegetation in fresh water marshes.

**Spotted Crake**
May not be quite as rare as we think, but certainly very hard to see. A few breed each year, deep in marshes. Strange "whiplash" call. Looks like a short-billed, spotty Water Rail (page 75).

**Corncrake**
Scarce summer visitor, breeding only in the western isles of Scotland and in Ireland. Very occasionally turns up at coastal sites on migration. Call both distinctive and relentless "crex crex".

**Stone Curlew**
A scarce summer visitor. Small breeding population restricted to sandy heaths and adjacent farmland in East Anglia. and Dorset/Hampshire. It is shy, secretive, and perfectly camouflaged, especially when it freezes, but once seen it is unmistakable.

## Red-necked Phalarope

The characteristic feature of both the Red-necked and Grey Phalarope (see below) is that they habitually feed by swimming on water, spinning round and round picking off flies. Small breeding population is restricted to Shetland, and occasionally seen farther south on autumn passage on fresh water, but rarely more than one or two.

Breeding plumage (above), non-breeding (above right), juvenile (right).

## Grey Phalarope

Occurs around our coasts and occasionally inland almost exclusively in autumn, mainly in September and October, but possible any time in winter. They will almost invariably be swimming on the water. The phalarope's dark cap and black eye patch is often surprisingly noticeable. Heavier bill distinguishes a Grey from Red-necked. Can be very tame.

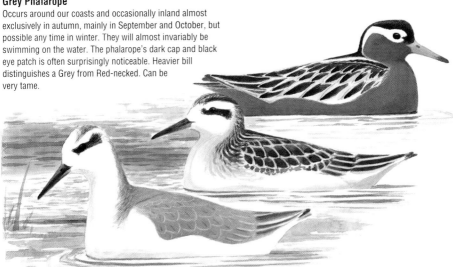

Juvenile (centre) and non-breeding (above). Pale grey upperparts variably flecked with darker feathers, and white underparts. These are the only likely plumages to be seen in Britain.

Does not breed in Britain and – as far as I know – breeding plumage (top) has never been seen here. A pity, since it is very striking, with totally orange underparts.

### Long-tailed Skua
The rarest of the British Skuas. Does not breed here, but some years quite large numbers are seen on spring migration, mainly off the Hebrides and other northern seawatch points. Alas, not always seen with long tail.

### Rock Dove
Feral pigeons (page 132) can look exactly like Rock Doves – they descended from them originally. Genuine wild birds probably occur only on the coastal areas of western Scotland and Ireland. Note the pale rump.

### Glaucous Gull
**Non-breeding** (left) and **breeding** (right). A "white-winged" gull from the Arctic. The larger of the white-winged gulls. Can be as big as a Great Black-back. Note the heavy beak. Juveniles are biscuit-coloured, second-years almost pure white, adults like large Herring Gull.

### Iceland Gull
**Non-breeding** (left) and **breeding** (right) More petite than Glaucous (usually smaller than Herring Gull) with smaller bill and kindlier face! The same range of plumages as Glaucous. Generally the scarcer of the two species.

### Snowy Owl

An extremely rare Arctic visitor. A pair used to breed on the Shetland Island of Fetlar, but now it is only sporadically recorded. Compare Barn Owl (page 137). Snowy is much bigger.

### Ring-necked Parakeet

This exotic has now been accepted as an honorary British bird. Several colonies are thriving, mainly in the south of England. Especially in winter, flocks may contain several hundred birds.

### Hoopoe

Hoopoes have very occasionally bred in Britain, but they mainly occur as scarce migrants, usually at coastal sites in spring or autumn, most likely in the south and east. Beware confusion with Jay. Hoopoe flies like a huge butterfly.

### Bluethroat

A scarce passage migrant at coastal locations, either in May (especially on the east and north-east coasts) or in September. In autumn, birds are likely to be in dull juvenile plumage, without the Union Jack waistcoat.

### Wryneck

Most likely to be seen on migration – especially on east coast and in Northern Isles – in spring, and less commonly in autumn. Technically, this is a small woodpecker, but more often seen on the ground or on stone walls.

There are many species of rare warblers that occur very occasionally in Britain as vagrants. Finding and identifying them is a tricky business! On the next two pages are a few that are at least slightly more frequent. Your best chance of seeing any of them is at a coastal migration hot spot in the autumn. With any luck at all, there will be other birders in the area to corroborate – or contradict – your sighting!

**Icterine Warbler** (left)
**Melodious Warbler** (above)
They have jizz of the Reed types (see Reed Warbler) but plumage is more akin to Willow Warbler. Rather slow movers. Best distinction is wing length - Icterine has a longer pointed wing.

**Pallas's Warbler**
Pallas's in particular may occur quite late in the year. As small as a Goldcrest and a mass of yellowy stripes, most notably on the crown and across the rump.

**Yellow-browed Warbler**
Like Pallas's, petite and agile, and most likely at coastal locations in autumn. Yellow-browed has a loud thin call "tsooeeet", like Coal Tit, which may draw attention to the bird.

**Barred Warbler**
A clumsy slow-moving warbler, clearly related to Blackcap and Garden Warbler. Often found in their company. Only breeding birds are barred - we don't see them like this in Britain in autumn. Imagine it without bars!

**These three are localized breeders:**

## Cetti's Warbler
The original elusive little brown skulking bird! A small number breed in marshy locations in southern England. Song: very loud and fruity: "chip chewicha weecha" (and variants). Once heard, easily recognized resident.

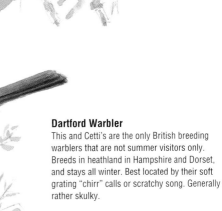

## Dartford Warbler
This and Cetti's are the only British breeding warblers that are not summer visitors only. Breeds in heathland in Hampshire and Dorset, and stays all winter. Best located by their soft grating "chirr" calls or scratchy song. Generally rather skulky.

## Marsh Warbler
Extremely similar to Reed Warbler and difficult to identify by plumage. Song is very different: a rich jumble of notes, incorporating mimicry of other species. Very scarce breeder in the south and scarce spring migrant in the northern isles.

## Red-breasted Flycatcher

Another rare migrant seen very rarely in breeding plumage. Far more likely in autumn. Similar to a female Pied Flycatcher, but note the lack of white wing bar. Imagine this without the red breast. Beware moulty Stonechats and young Robins.

## Crested Tit

Lives only in the mature pine forests of Scotland and, even there, it can be hard to find! Outside breeding season, birds may join other species and rove a little.

## Golden Oriole

**Female** (left) and **male** (right). Summer visitors and small numbers breed, mainly in poplar plantations in East Anglia. A few also turn up on migration, most commonly in late spring. Song distinctive – a fluty whistle. Beware glimpses of Green Woodpeckers.

## Red-backed Shrike

**Male** (left) and **female** (right). Probably extinct as a breeding bird in Britain, but still occurs in small numbers as a migrant. Your best bet is probably the Northern Isles in May or early June.

### Chough
Resident on rocky coasts, in a few places in western Britain, Ireland and the Isle of Man. Even where Choughs are present, you are unlikely to see more than a dozen or so together. Like a Jackdaw with curved red bill and "sneezing" call.

### Scottish Crossbill
Defined as a separate species within the last twenty years. Confined to northern Scotland. Almost impossible to differentiate from Common Crossbill (page 215) in the field: Scottish has a larger beak.

### Lapland Bunting
Scarce visitor, mainly to coastal locations, in autumn and very occasionally in spring. Small numbers may winter in some years on short-cropped terrain. Has very occasionally bred in Scotland, but usually seen in winter-type plumage.

### Cirl Bunting
**Male** (foreground) and **female**. Very rare in Britain, breeding only in a few rural areas in south west England. Similar to Yellowhammer (page 220), but male has striking face pattern: black crown, eyeline and chin. Female has brown rump.

### Ortolan Bunting
A few occur in spring (May) and slightly more in autumn (September). Typical bunting, with white outer tail feathers, distinctive male, but drab female and juvenile. All show white orbital ring.

# FURTHER ACTION

Many bird books include a page of 'suggested further reading'. I am a little loath to do this as, frankly, there are an awful lot of excellent books available on all aspects of birds and birdwatching, and – more to the point – new ones are being published all the time. What I will do, however, is suggest that you subscribe to at least two of the various bird magazines on the market. Mind you, I'm not going to suggest which two! Have a look at them all and decide which ones best suit your taste. In fact, all or any of these magazines will provide you with the extra information you may need about new books, birdlines, pager services, optical equipment, and so on.

Above all, I do recommend – nay exhort – you to join a number of conservation organizations. I really believe that anyone who takes pleasure from watching birds is honour bound to help protect them. Please do so.

## MAGAZINES

*Birdwatch*
From newsagents, or by subscription from Birdwatch (Subs Dept.), Fulham House, Goldsworth Road, Woking, Surrey GU21 ILY.

*Birdwatching*
From newsagents, or from Birdwatching (Subscriptions), Tower Publishing Services Ltd., Tower House, Sovereign Park, Market Harborough, Leicestershire LE 16 9EF.

*Birding World*
By subscription from Stonerunner, Coast Road, Cley Next the Sea, Holt, Norfolk NR25 7RZ.

*British Birds*
By subscription from Fountains, Park Lane, Blunham, Bedford MK44 3NJ.

## CONSERVATION ORGANISATIONS

**RSPB** (The Royal Society for the Protection of Birds)
The Lodge, Sandy, Bedfordshire SG19 2DI.
Tel: 01767 680551

**YOC** (Young Ornithologists Club)
The Lodge, Sandy, Bedfordshire SGI9 2DI.
Tel: 01767 680551

**BTO** (British Trust for Ornithology)
The National Centre for Ornithology, The Nunnery, Thetford, Norfolk IP24 2PU.

**The Wildfowl and Wetlands Trust**
Slimbridge, Gloucestershire GL2 7BT.

**The Wildlife Trusts**
The Green, Witham Park, Waterside South, Lincoln LN5 7JR.
Tel 01522 544400 for information about your local County Trust.

# INDEX

# INDEX

# INDEX